# A manager's guide
# to the antitrust laws

# A manager's guide to the antitrust laws

## Edward A. Matto

A Division of American Management Associations

**Library of Congress Cataloging in Publication Data**

Matto, Edward A
    A manager's guide to the antitrust laws.

    Includes index.
    1. Antitrust law—United States.    I. Title.
KF1649.M34        343.73'072        79-54843
ISBN 0-8144-5541-7

*To my wife, Michele, and our children,*
*Holly, E.J., and Kevin*

# Preface

A common error made by many business managers is to assume that the antitrust laws do not apply to them or their companies because of company size, managerial position in the company, or the type of industry involved. It is too late to reassess that thinking when your company is writing a check for several hundred thousand or even several million dollars to satisfy an antitrust treble damage judgment or when one of your officers is being escorted off to jail.

The purpose of this book is to give you, the non-lawyer business manager, a basic understanding of the antitrust laws in nonlegal terms so that you and your company may be better able both to comply with the laws and to recognize when you should consult your company's attorney on antitrust questions. A basic understanding of the antitrust laws and their underlying philosophy is the first, and probably the most important, step necessary in any company's antitrust compliance program.

Violation of the Sherman Act is now a felony. The adverse impact on those who violate the antitrust laws is tremendous, so it is vital that you, as an employee and/or officer of the company, have a basic understanding of the laws. However, when high prices may be construed as evidence of a monopoly, stable prices as evidence of price fixing, and low prices as evidence of an illegal attempt to drive a competitor out of business, it is often very difficult to know what is and what is not permissible.

This book is not intended to turn you into an attorney or make you an antitrust expert; no summary of the antitrust laws could do that. The clear-cut violations may be obvious, but the more common questions often are not so clear. They may concern borderline activities and require legal advice. Hopefully, this book will provide an understanding of the basic rationale underlying the antitrust laws and the types of activities that are illegal or that might be suspect. The book will concentrate on the federal antitrust laws, but much of what is covered would also apply to many of the various state antitrust laws.

Most of the book could be construed as providing "thou shalt not's." That is because the antitrust laws themselves have basically been construed that way by the courts. These chapters should, therefore, help fix in your mind some of the limitations of the antitrust laws and how the laws might apply to various aspects of your company's business. They may raise questions pertinent to your particular business and thereby signal that you should take the time to assess the questions from an antitrust viewpoint and possibly consult with your company's attorney regarding them.

The book is not an antitrust answer book; it is intended to assist you in complying with the complex, and often vague and misunderstood, antitrust laws and possibly save you and your company lots of grief and a great deal of money. Since it is directed to business managers rather than attorneys, it does not contain a large number of case citations. Too many such footnotes would slow down the reading and reduce the use of the book by non-lawyers. You may notice some repetition of certain explanations in different parts of the book. That is intentional. It is hoped that the book will be used by the business person as a reference book on particular questions as well as a source of general antitrust knowledge, and therefore it was felt that certain explanations should be included in several different sections of the book.

I want to acknowledge several people whose various contributions helped make this book possible. My wife, Michele, provided continuous moral support as well as a detailed review of the manuscript. Her suggestions and comments from the viewpoint of a non-lawyer business person were invaluable.

Nathan P. Eimer (of the law firm of Sidley & Austin in Chicago), a fellow member of the antitrust bar, provided extremely useful comments on the manuscript from the viewpoint of a practicing antitrust lawyer. The dedication, skill, and positive attitude of Marjorie Davis in preparing the manuscript is also greatly appreciated.

EDWARD A. MATTO

# Contents

# 1

# An overview
# of the antitrust laws

## Coverage of the antitrust laws

The antitrust laws can affect your company when it acts as a
competitor, supplier, franchiser, franchisee, distributor, agent,
or purchaser. They can affect your company irrespective of its
size—whether it is small, medium, or large. They can affect
many of your employees: the chairman of the board, the president and other executives, sales personnel, purchasing personnel, marketing personnel, credit personnel, and many others.

With the few exceptions given in Chapter 12, there is no
escaping the coverage of the antitrust laws. The enterprises
and entrepreneurs involved in antitrust litigation in one fashion or another over the past several years include folding car-
tons, corrugated containers, baking, architectural hardware,
taxi service, gasoline dealers, dictation equipment distributors,
land-surveying services, automobile dealers, construction
firms, oil, gas meters, liquor, wood-burning stoves, energy,
pharmaceuticals, electrical equipment, foods, footwear, grocery, towing services, ice cream franchisers, fast food franchisers, medical doctors, real estate brokers, professional football,
cement producers, dog racing, and computer companies. The
list is almost endless.

Various antitrust statutes are enforced at the federal, state, and local governmental levels. Suits for treble damages are brought by various private companies and individuals and often by states on behalf of all their individual citizens who may have suffered damages as a result of antitrust violations.

The antitrust laws can affect many different aspects of a business: pricing, marketing, sales, purchasing, amount or types of ingredients or raw materials, use of agents, membership in trade or professional associations, participation in codes of ethics, and franchise and distributor arrangements. It is obvious, therefore, that anyone in your organization who has a role in any of those functions should have a basic understanding of the antitrust laws so that he may attempt to fully comply with the antitrust laws.*

If you, as a business manager, had an opportunity to make a decision that would permit a $100,000 tax deduction to be taken by your company and thereby create approximately $50,000 of additional income on your company's profit and loss statement for that year, you would take it. And probably very often you or others in your company do consider the tax consequences of certain decisions. You may even seek advice from tax experts in an attempt to maximize your tax deductions and tax credits and thereby maximize your company's net income after taxes.

Now if you had an opportunity to make a decision that would prevent a $300,000 decrease in income, you would certainly take that, too—if you knew how to prevent such a loss! And that is what you can know when you have a basic understanding of the antitrust laws. Since private parties damaged by violation of the federal antitrust laws can collect three times their damages, any company that is proved liable for an antitrust violation can be required to pay three times the proven damages to the plaintiffs. Thus if private plaintiffs were damaged in the amount of $100,000, as by the excess price charged in a price-fixing case, the defendant would be liable for $300,000. Also, in many situations, two-thirds of the payment

---

*It is equally obvious that the person in need of the understanding may be female, but the English language has no suitable neutral pronoun. In lieu of one, "he" rather than the awkward "he or she" will be used.

is not tax deductible; it comes off the bottom line of your financial statement.

## Your company's rights under the antitrust laws

Your company has certain rights under the antitrust laws. It is entitled to expect conduct in compliance with those laws from competitors, suppliers, customers, franchisers, franchisees, and/or distributors. If your company is damaged as a result of a violation, then it is entitled to sue for treble damages plus costs and reasonable attorneys' fees.

Those rights are available to your company without regard to size. No matter if your company is the smallest in or the giant of the industry, it is entitled to expect from others conduct that complies with the antitrust laws. However, there are certain situations in which, because of its dominant position in the industry, one company is considered fair game by its smaller competitors, whose conduct would be taken as evidence of an antitrust violation if engaged in by the giant. For example, a small competitor can often offer discounts or very low prices in an attempt to steal customers from the giant. If the dominant company used such tactics, it might be accused of attempting to illegally obtain or retain a monopoly position in the industry or in a particular market or product.

Your company's rights include the expectation that your competitors, suppliers, and others will conform to the requirements of the antitrust laws as set forth in this book. If they do not, then you may have a cause of action and a right to collect three times your damages, to seek an injunction prohibiting such conduct, to seek to void certain contracts, or to obtain whatever the appropriate remedy might be. For example, if your suppliers are fixing prices on materials sold to your company and you have been damaged, you have a right to sue to collect treble damages and to obtain an injunction prohibiting any further such conduct.

## The basic purpose of the antitrust laws

The basic purpose of the antitrust laws is to preserve the concept of free and open competition—the basic economic philosophy upon which our country was formed. The antitrust laws were passed to promote competition and to prevent anticompetitive conduct that would conflict with the basic economic philosophy. Thus the antitrust laws embody this country's national policy of recognizing the benefit to society of a competitive economy. They are basically directed at anticompetitive agreements and conduct that unfairly restrict competition.

The first antitrust laws were passed to break up business trusts such as those in oil, sugar, and tobacco. There was national concern over the concentration of so much economic power in the hands of a few and a national conclusion that such trusts were economically and politically unsound. After several years of congressional discussing, proposing, revising, and fighting, the national concern was transformed into the Sherman Act. Several states, at the same time or shortly thereafter, passed similar and in some cases identical legislation; today most states have some form of antitrust laws.

As business structures became more varied and more complex and as the conduct of businesses became more sophisticated, the emphasis and scope of the antitrust laws were broadened to cover more and varied activities, activities that were unknown and unanticipated by the Congress that passed the Sherman Act in 1890. Today we have "mom and pop" stores, family-owned factories, franchise systems, distributor networks, regionally concentrated industries, national companies, multinational conglomerates, and many varied professions.

> Antitrust laws in general, and the Sherman Act in particular, are the Magna Carta of free enterprise. They are as important to the preservation of economic freedom and our free-enterprise system as the Bill of Rights is to the protection of our fundamental personal freedoms. And the freedom guaranteed each and every business, no matter how small, is the freedom to compete—to assert with vigor, imagination, devotion, and ingenuity whatever economic muscle it can muster.[1]

The restraints of trade prohibited by the Sherman, Clayton, Robinson-Patman, and Federal Trade Commission Acts vary somewhat with the statute, but they apply to agreements and conduct that, basically, would unreasonably lessen competition. In other words, they apply to an agreement or conduct that has been deemed to be anticompetitive rather than procompetitive. The purpose of review by a court, then, is to determine whether particular facts exist to find that certain agreements and/or conduct occurred and/or to form a judgment about the competitive significance of the restraint.

Because the purpose of the antitrust laws is to create a fair, competitive arena and to set up some basic rules to assure compliance with the laws, effective and responsible enforcement can benefit both businesses and consumers. Businesses benefit because they are then the recipients of competitively priced raw materials and other supplies, are not the victims of market tampering by their competitors, and are given an opportunity to operate in a competitive arena without being victimized by artificial manipulation of the competitive process by someone in their distribution chain or by competitors. Consumers benefit because they can purchase products that are priced competitively and therefore as low as is practical.

### Federal and state antitrust statutes

The pertinent federal statutes, the language of which is set out in Appendix A, are:

- The Sherman Act, which prohibits, in general terms, agreements, combinations, and conspiracies in restraint of trade (such as price fixing, allocation of customers or territories, refusals to deal, unreasonable restraints), monopolization, and a conspiracy or an attempt to monopolize.

- The Clayton Act, which basically prohibits a lease, sale, or a contract for sale of any product upon the condition, agreement, or understanding that the buyer will not use or deal in the products of a competitor of the seller or lessor when such an arrangement may substantially lessen competition or tend to create a monopoly. The Act thereby covers exclusive dealing, requirements contracts, and tying arrangements. It also covers anticompetitive mergers and acquisitions.

- The Robinson-Patman Act (actually part of the Clayton Act), which covers discrimination in prices, brokerage fees, and promotional allowances and services.

• The Federal Trade Commission Act, which prohibits unfair methods of competition (including most of the conduct covered by the Sherman and Clayton Acts) and unfair or deceptive acts or practices.

In addition to the federal statutes, as mentioned earlier, most states have some form of antitrust statute. Because many of the state laws are construed in the same way as the federal law, conduct that would violate the federal statutes could also violate a state's laws. Many states, through their attorneys general, are becoming very active in enforcing their antitrust laws, as well as suing under the federal statutes for treble damages on behalf of the state and its agencies and/or its individual citizens.

Thus you need also be concerned about state antitrust laws. In this book, discussion and reference to "antitrust laws" primarily covers the federal antitrust laws; but when state statutes are construed as consistent with the federal statutes, the discussion is applicable to the state statutes as well. Whether the state laws are interpreted similarly to the federal statutes or somewhat differently, you obviously must be aware of their existence.

When the Sherman Act was passed in 1890, primarily because of the various large trusts that had been forming, the concentration of a particular industry in the hands of a few disturbed the country as it often does today. The consensus then, as now, was that our economic system works best through competition and that any attempt by a business to grow other than through acumen and normal practices should be prohibited. Thus, Section 2 of the Sherman Act states that "every person who shall monopolize, or attempt to monopolize, or combine or conspire . . . to monopolize . . . shall be deemed guilty" of violating the Act.

However, the Sherman Act was passed with language much broader than was necessary to cover the trusts and the anticompetitive means to accomplish domination by the trusts. Section 1 of the Sherman Act reads, in pertinent part, "every contract, combination or conspiracy in restraint of trade" is illegal. Thus the language could be interpreted as prohibiting all business contracts, since any contract would restrain trade to some extent. However, the courts have generally interpreted section 1 as prohibiting "unreasonable" restraints of trade. In other words, the antitrust laws are intended to promote competition, and only the agreements that unreasonably restrain trade and thereby are anticompetitive rather than procompetitive are illegal.

The courts have basically carved out two tests against which to review various agreements or conduct. The first is the *per se category,* and the courts have held that agreements falling within it will always be unreasonable restraints of trade and therefore should always be identified as illegal.

By the *rule-of-reason test,* any agreement that is not per se illegal is reviewed in its particular factual setting to determine if it is unreasonably restrictive on competition and is therefore anticompetitive.

The Clayton Act was passed in 1914, and it has since been amended several times. It specifically covers such activity as tying arrangements, requirements contracts, and exclusive-dealing contracts. It also prohibits certain mergers between and acquisitions of corporations if the effect may be to substantially lessen competition or tend to create a monopoly. The Act contains other prohibitive sections that deal with such areas as interlocking directorates of certain banking and other financial corporations and certain matters involving common carriers.

Congress also passed in 1914 the Federal Trade Commission Act, which created the Federal Trade Commission (FTC) and authorized it to enforce the Act. As amended, the FTC Act prohibits, in pertinent part, "unfair methods of competition" and "unfair or deceptive acts or practices." "Unfair methods of competition" is the language which covers antitrust violations. "Unfair or deceptive acts or practices" covers unfair trade practices, which basically involve consumer protection questions. The FTC Act is to be enforced by the FTC; it does not give to private parties any right of action under its provisions.

The Clayton Act was amended in 1936 by the Robinson-Patman Act to prevent discrimination in prices, brokers' fees, allowances, services, and facilities. The basic intent at the time was to prevent large buyers from exercising their buying leverage to obtain price and other concessions not available to smaller purchasers and not supported by any real cost savings to the seller.

### The need for a basic understanding of the antitrust laws

The antitrust laws govern the conduct of and relationships between parties in the vertical chain of distribution and also competitors on a horizontal level. Price fixing, although the most commonly known, is only one of the prohibited activities. And even the term "price fixing" is a lot broader than you might think. For example, it is applied to agreements among competitors on discounts, base prices, rebates, freight rates, credit terms, ceiling prices, and minimum prices and restrictions on bonuses, gifts, or other sales terms. It also covers agreements between a supplier and a purchaser on the resale price to be charged, on minimum or maximum prices to be charged, and on discounts, rebates, credit terms, and other sales terms to be offered.

A basic understanding of the antitrust laws is important to you and to your company, no matter what its size. There are many, many situations in which your company's attorney should be consulted in the hope of preventing future problems. Although many do's and don'ts can be identified—and many of them will be identified throughout the book—there are other situations in which the determination of permissible conduct hinges on that vague notion of what is "reasonable."

After you have a basic understanding of the antitrust laws, you most likely will develop a sense for many business relationships and conduct and whether a particular situation is permitted under the antitrust laws or needs further review. It is this sense that can be invaluable to your company and to you. It can help avoid expensive problems and keep you out of jail.

### REFERENCE

1. *United States v. Topco Associates, Inc.*, 405 U.S. 596, 610 (1972).

# 2

# Consequences of violation of the antitrust laws

There are many possible consequences, to your company and to you, of a violation of the antitrust laws. Naturally, they vary with the type of violation. But they also vary with whether a criminal or civil suit is brought or both are brought, whether suit is brought by the government or by private parties or by both, the extent of involvement of particular parties, the length of time the violation occurred, and whether it is the first anti-trust violation by the defendant. Generally speaking, however, the following are some of the possible adverse consequences that you and your company would be facing.

### Jail sentence and/or fines

For a criminal violation under the Sherman Act, a corporation can be fined up to $1 million and an individual can be sentenced to prison for up to 3 years and/or fined up to $100,000. Many states also have criminal penalties for violation of their state statutes. The penalties vary from state to state, but in many instances they also include large fines and/or jail sentences.

The trend in the courts and the emphasis by the United States Department of Justice is on heavier fines and longer jail sentences. In an attempt to obtain increased fines and sentences, the Antitrust Division of the Department of Justice has recommended sentencing guidelines. They are discussed in Chapter 11, Government Enforcement of the Antitrust Laws.

### Treble damages by individual plaintiffs

Private parties, including consumers, have a right to sue for the damages they suffered as a result of an alleged antitrust violation. If the private parties prove an antitrust violation and prove that they suffered damage as a result of it, they are entitled to *three times* their actual damages plus costs and reasonable attorneys' fees. Damages can therefore run from thousands into hundreds of millions of dollars. Furthermore, the participants in an alleged agreement, combination, or conspiracy are jointly and severally liable, and any one participant is legally liable for all the damages of the persons injured by the violation. (See Joint and Several Liability, in Chapter 13.)

A treble damage action can be brought by a state, municipality, or other non-federal governmental entity that may have suffered damages as a result of its having purchased the particular product or service involved. The plaintiffs could include, and on occasion have included, company employees as individual defendants in treble damage actions.

### Class action by damaged purchasers

The law permits a private party, if certain conditions are met, to sue on its own behalf and as a representative on behalf of all potential members of the same group or class similarly situated as the plaintiff. (See Class Actions; Notices of Participation, Chapter 13.) The class action procedure provides that if liability and damages are shown, then the defendants are liable to each of the members of the class—except those who have elected earlier to be excluded from the class—for treble their proven damages. In class action antitrust cases, there may be several classes suing or one class encompassing all potentially injured parties. Obviously, the financial risk to any company subject to such antitrust class action litigation can be tremendous.

### Parens patriae suits

The various state attorneys general have authority to bring actions on behalf of all natural persons within their particular states who might have been damaged as the result of violation of the Sherman Act. This is referred to as *parens patriae* authority. (See *Parens Patriae* Suits by States, Chapter 13.) Thus, for example, a state attorney general could bring a suit alleging the fixing of prices on a particular consumer product and seek treble damages on behalf of all individual consumers of his state who might have purchased the product. The amount of money that could be involved in such a lawsuit begins to multiply, especially if it is compounded by several suits on behalf of consumers of other states or if, in addition, other class action suits are brought by particular classes of purchasers.

### Injunctive relief

Another remedy often available is injunctive relief, whereby a court order prohibits or requires certain contractual provisions, type of conduct, or type of business arrangement. An injunction could require your company to refrain from agreeing on prices, refrain from selling at "unreasonably low prices," restructure its distribution system or franchise arrangement or void certain provisions of it, terminate a particular product line, share certain of its technical know-how or available raw materials with its competitors or potential competitors, sell off certain assets or a line of business, or refrain from acquiring a particular company or line of business. The actual thrust of the court-issued injunction would naturally depend upon what remedy was sought in the lawsuit, what conduct was involved, and what remedy the court determined was appropriate.

The prohibitions may put your company in a less favorable position than its competitors and thereby create adverse business conditions for it. Before it could deviate from the substantive requirements of the decree or court order, it would have to go back into court and attempt to obtain a revised order. Conduct of the business in a manner inconsistent with the consent decree or court order must be covered by a modified consent decree or court order reissued by the court.

A consent decree is an agreed-upon court order; it is also referred to as a consent order or consent judgment. It is agreed to by the Federal Trade Commission, the Antitrust Division of the Department of Justice, or some other enforcement agency.

The order or decree typically requires that copies be distributed to various company employees, perhaps including each new employee in a position covered by the order or decree. In addition, depending upon the thrust of the order or decree, there may be a requirement to distribute copies to one's customers, suppliers, franchisees, distributors, and so on.

Many orders and decrees require that annual reports be filed with the appropriate governmental enforcement agency to assure compliance with the order or decree. Further, there usually is a provision which permits the agency to view the company's books and records as they pertain to the subject of the order or decree in order to assure itself of compliance.

### Suit against individual employees

Many antitrust suits could, and some suits do, include as defendants the employees who allegedly participated in the conspiracy alleged in the lawsuit. That is true of both civil and criminal suits. Criminal suits carry a possible jail sentence and heavy fine; civil suits usually seek monetary compensation for alleged damages from the individual as well as from the other corporate defendants.

Many states do not permit a corporation to pay for the defense of an employee who has knowingly committed a crime, and therefore the employee may need to pay for his own legal defense in any criminal case. Most states, however, permit company reimbursement for attorneys' fees and other expenses incurred by an employee who is found innocent.

Normally the employee would obtain his own counsel. He would need to work with his attorney in preparation for his own defense as well as work with the company's attorneys in preparation of the company defense (to the extent there was no conflict between the two defenses). The criminal case, as well as any civil cases, would occupy most of the employee's thoughts; it would interfere with his family life and routine; and it would lessen his contribution to the company during the period of the litigation, which might be several years.

## Emotional effect upon involved employees

The emotional drain on an individual who is named as a defendant is tremendous, and so is it on an employee who is only alleged to be a coconspirator or who was working in the particular area under question. Certain of such employees may be subpoenaed by a grand jury for their depositions in the litigation and/or for testifying at trial. Even if they are not defendants or alleged coconspirators, the emotional effect on them will be great.

## Cost in time and money

Any lawsuit entails cost in time and money to all parties. That is especially true of antitrust litigation, which generally involves many people, may have complex economic, legal, and factual aspects, and may continue for several years. Even prior to the filing of any criminal case or government civil suit, there might be a grand jury investigation or a formal government civil investigation that would require much time of and impose emotional drain on the employees involved. The employees might be subpoenaed to testify. Also, certain documents might be subpoenaed, and they and others that might be helpful at trial would have to be reviewed with various employees by the attorneys.

A company can expect, either as a plaintiff in a civil action or a defendant in either a criminal or civil action, to commit much employee time to assisting the attorneys in their litigation. The time is spent in answering the attorneys' inquiries, retrieving information, abstracting data, locating documents, responding to document subpoenas, producing documents, answering interrogatories, being interviewed, preparing for depositions, having depositions taken, preparing to be witnesses at trial, and attending and testifying at trial.

It is possible that you will need to hire one or more

experts in economics, your industry, or an area or field that pertains to your lawsuit such as particular government agencies or regulations. (Examples of the latter are wage-price and import-export regulations.) Experts, like attorneys, are expensive. The expert will often need to devote a great portion of his time to prepare for the lawsuit and for his deposition, and such expenditure of time becomes company expense.

And, of course, attorneys' fees can become very large. Antitrust cases typically demand much attorney time to be defended or pursued properly. Your attorneys need to know your company and your industry extremely well if they are to present a well-prepared case. That usually means that more than one attorney is involved, as well as paralegals, law clerks, and other assistants. Each added person multiplies the expense to your company.

In addition, there are other expenses: copying, which can run up into hundreds of thousands of sheets of paper; travel by employees, attorneys, and experts; computer time if the information being accumulated is stored in a computer for easy retrieval, as it sometimes is when a case involves hundreds of thousands of documents; long-distance telephone calls; outside clerical help to number, sort, and categorize documents; and many other expenses that can not be foreseen. And if you lose a private civil antitrust suit, the federal statutes, as well as some state statutes, require that you pay the other party its costs plus reasonable attorneys' fees. Costs would not include all of the above, but they may include some of them. The big expense, naturally, would be the attorneys' fees.

### Bad publicity

Just having an antitrust suit filed against your company can result in much unwanted publicity. It seems that such terms as "antitrust," "price fixing," and "monopolization" are newsworthy and are promptly picked up by the press. That may mean front-page articles in local newspapers and even in national and financial newspapers. Trade or professional association or industry periodicals may carry the story; consumer-oriented periodicals may pick it up; and radio and TV will often give it coverage as well.

It usually doesn't go away after the first barrage either, especially if it's a criminal case or a large civil damage suit. It keeps rearing its ugly head throughout the period of the litigation and sometimes for years afterward. In fact, the publicity could begin with rumors concerning a grand jury or other government investigation or the anticipated filing of an antitrust suit by a private party.

There may also be publicity when the criminal indictment is filed, when the initial pleas of innocence are given, when any later plea is given, and while the trial is in progress. In a civil suit, publicity may come when the civil action is filed, when the court makes rulings of any significance, when in a class action suit the court authorizes the sending of notices to all the potential members of that class (which typically includes the customers of the defendants) to inform them of the lawsuit and the option to participate as class members, and during the trial.

The point is that bad publicity can begin very early in an antitrust investigation and continue throughout the entire litigation and often for years thereafter.

### Tax consequences

The federal tax law, section 162 of the Internal Revenue Code of 1954, as amended, prohibits the deduction of any fine paid in a criminal antitrust case. In addition, section 162(g) reads as follows:

> If in a criminal proceeding a taxpayer is convicted of a violation of the antitrust laws or his plea of guilty or nolo contendere to an indictment or information charging such a violation is entered or accepted in such a proceeding, no deduction shall be allowed . . . for two-thirds of any amount paid or incurred—(1) on any judgment for damages entered against the taxpayer under section 4 of . . . [The Clayton Act], on account of such violation or any related violation of the antitrust laws which occurred prior to date of the final judgment of such conviction, or (2) in settlement of any action brought under such section 4 on account of such violation or related violation.

The section 4 of the Clayton Act that is referred to above is the provision that permits private parties to sue for treble damages under the antitrust laws, both the Sherman Act and the Clayton Act. Thus any criminal fine levied against a corporation would be nondeductible. For example, if the maximum corporate fine of $1 million were levied, it would come directly off the bottom line of your profit and loss statement as a nontax-deductible charge against income.

Likewise, two-thirds of any amount paid as a judgment or as a settlement in a civil antitrust action is not tax deductible if the civil action is based upon the conduct involved in the criminal antitrust case. Therefore, if your company were faced with a criminal antitrust case and a civil damage action based upon the same allegations were to follow, it could not deduct two-thirds of any civil judgment entered or settlement made once that civil action was filed if it had entered a plea of guilty or nolo contendere or were found guilty in the criminal action. That two-thirds would come directly off the bottom line of your profit and loss statement as a non-tax-deductible charge against income. There are obviously several legal and factual questions that would need to be resolved whenever this question arose; but if the civil and criminal cases were based on the same allegations, section 162(g) would apply.

If your company is involved in a criminal antitrust case and is aware that a civil damage action may arise out of the same alleged facts, it may want to attempt to negotiate a settlement of the civil claim prior to the filing of the civil damage action. It will thereby preserve the argument that, since the civil action had not been filed, it is entitled to a full deduction of such settlement. Naturally, there are factors other than the tax consequences that would enter into any decision on whether to settle before a civil damage action was filed or defend any such litigation in court.

### Effect on financial statements

As described under Tax Consequences, above, there can be a direct effect on the bottom line of your profit and loss statements from a tax standpoint. In addition to the tax considerations, the company's independent public accountants may feel it necessary to qualify its statements until the antitrust suit is resolved or a particular damage award is resolved on appeal.

For example, if there is an antitrust judgment against a corporation for a large sum that would have a substantial adverse impact upon the company's financial condition, the accountants may decline to certify the statement until the amount of the damage is ascertained either on appeal of the decision or through some negotiated settlement of the amount to be paid. In other situations, the accountants may feel it necessary to at least footnote the litigation.

# 3

# Basic concepts and terms

To have an understanding of the antitrust laws, you need a basic familiarity with certain terms and concepts that permeate the antitrust field. The following explanations should further your knowledge of the antitrust laws and their application to your particular business. The basic purpose of the antitrust laws has been discussed in Chapter 1.

## Application to businesses and professions

The antitrust laws apply to all businesses and professions with these few exceptions: labor unions, insurance companies, agricultural cooperatives, regulated industries (to some extent), baseball, certain state governmental actions, and certain conduct to petition the government. Even the exceptions apply only to certain conduct of the entities involved. (See Chapter 12, Exemptions to the Antitrust Laws.)

Thus it is clear that it is very hard to escape antitrust coverage. The antitrust laws apply to all interstate commercial activity and include both profit and nonprofit companies, corporations, trade and professional associations, partnerships, sole proprietorships, and individuals (for example, employees). They apply to all types of industries, large and small, and all professions—medicine, law, engineering, accounting, and so on. However, certain professional conduct might be deemed legal that would be illegal for a business to engage in. The U.S. Supreme Court has said:

> The fact that a restraint operates upon a profession as distinguished from a business is, of course, relevant in determining whether that particular restraint violates the Sherman Act. It would be unrealistic to view the practice of professions as interchangeable with other business activities, and automatically to apply to the profession antitrust concepts which originated in other areas. The public service aspect, and other features of the professions, may require that a particular practice, which could properly be viewed as a violation of the Sherman Act in another context, be treated differently. . . .[1]

Exactly what conduct might be legal when involving a profession rather than a business is unclear and will continue to be unclear for years. However, it is likely that the quoted language is primarily directed to the codes of ethics and rules to regulate the professions that have been implemented either by the professions themselves or by government agencies.

The federal antitrust laws apply to foreign businesses doing business in the United States. They also apply to American businesses doing business abroad and to foreign companies abroad when their conduct affects U.S. foreign commerce. That would include both exports and imports as well as activity solely occurring in a foreign country which affects U.S. foreign commerce. The practicalities of enforcing the U.S. antitrust laws against foreign companies conducting their business in foreign countries is a separate issue, albeit an important and practical one.

### Horizontal and vertical restraints

Horizontal agreement or conduct means agreement among or conduct involving competitors: entities and/or persons on the same level of the distribution chain whether they are retailers, wholesalers, manufacturers, franchisers, franchisees, distributors, licensors, or licensees.

Vertical agreement or conduct means agreement among or conduct involving entities on different levels of the distribution chain. An example is an agreement between a manufacturer and its distributor.

Thus a horizontal restraint of trade means an agreement among or conduct involving competitors that unreasonably restrains trade under the antitrust laws; that is, has been deemed anticompetitive. A vertical restraint of trade means an agreement among or conduct involving entities on different levels of the distribution chain that unreasonably restrains trade under the antitrust laws.

Important distinctions that are often made under the antitrust laws as to what is legal and what is illegal depend upon whether the agreement or conduct is horizontal or vertical. For example, many of the per se violations [see the discussion under Rule-of-Reason and Per Se Violation Tests, below] cover horizontal agreements and conduct rather than vertical agreements and conduct. Therefore, whether certain conduct is found to be horizontal or vertical can make a difference in determining if the conduct is deemed illegal.

For example, the U.S. Supreme Court, in a case involving Sealy, Inc., found that since the various Sealy "licensees" owned substantially all of the stock of Sealy, Inc., the manufacturer, any agreement between Sealy, Inc. and its licensees was in reality an agreement among the licensees on a horizontal level and therefore should be reviewed as a horizontal agreement. The licensees were viewed as using the manufacturer to implement any such horizontal agreements. Thus the allocation of exclusive territories to the licensees was a horizontal allocation of territories and per se illegal. The court stated the factual question as follows:

> Because this Court has distinguished between horizontal and vertical territorial limitations for purposes of the impact of the Sherman Act, it is first necessary to determine whether the territorial arrangements here are to be treated as the creature of the licensor, Sealy, or as the product of a horizontal arrangement among the licensees. . . .[2]

As the Sealy case indicates, the courts will generally look to the substance of the agreement or conduct involved and not merely to the form taken by the entities when attempting to determine whether certain conduct or an agreement is to be considered horizontal or vertical. In other words, if you walk like a duck, talk like a duck, and act like a duck, the court will label you a duck.

### Rule-of-reason and per se violation tests

The *rule-of-reason test* is the usual way to determine whether a particular agreement or particular conduct is illegal under section 1 of the Sherman Act. The courts also apply a rule-of-reason type of analysis to conduct and agreements being reviewed under the Clayton Act to determine if the conduct or agreement "may substantially lessen competition" and to any conduct or agreement being reviewed under the FTC Act as an "unfair method of competition." Thus an understanding of the rule-of-reason test will assist you in recognizing an agreement or conduct that might be suspect under the other antitrust statutes.

The rule-of-reason test means that an agreement or conduct that is shown to unreasonably restrain trade violates the antitrust laws. An unreasonable restraint is an agreement or conduct that is deemed to unreasonably restrict competition. The key is the word "unreasonable." Obviously, almost any contract will restrict competition to some extent. For example, a contract by company B to purchase 1,000 wedges from company A lessens competition, since company B will not be buying those wedges from company A's competition. However, under most circumstances, that would not be deemed illegal, because it would not be found to be an unreasonable restraint.

Using the rule-of-reason test, the court will look at all the pertinent facts to determine whether an agreement or a conduct is illegal. The court will analyze the purpose, effect, and other unique aspects of the business conduct or agreement in question as well as the power of the parties to implement the business conduct or agreement and often the role the conduct or agreement plays in the structure of the particular industry or profession.

The court must then determine, on balance, whether any procompetitive aspect of the business conduct or agreement in question outweighs any anticompetitive aspects. If so, the agreement or conduct will be held legal; if not, it will be held violative of the antitrust laws. That does give one an opportunity to argue that if such an agreement or conduct did exist (and often there is no question that it did), it did not unreasonably restrict competition. However, it also puts a high degree of vagueness into the system and often makes it difficult for a business person to determine whether certain actions would be illegal under the antitrust laws.

For example, the courts, in determining whether the conduct in question does violate the antitrust laws, may look at the industry as a whole, the length of any agreement in question, any substitutes for the raw materials or product involved, the percent of the market tied up by any agreement, and so forth, in determining the reasonableness of the restraint. Such determination is made by the courts on a case-by-case basis and is not subject to any more concrete definition.

The U.S. Supreme Court defined the rule-of-reason test as follows:

> The legality of an agreement or regulation cannot be determined by so simple a test as whether it restrains competition. Every agreement concerning trade, every regulation of trade, restrains. To bind, to restrain, is of their very essence. The true test of legality is whether the restraint imposed is such as merely regulates and perhaps thereby promotes competition or whether it is such as may suppress or even destroy competition. To determine that question the court must ordinarily consider the facts peculiar to the business to which the restraint is applied; its condition before and after the restraint was imposed; the nature of the restraint, and its effect, actual or probable. The history of the restraint, the evil believed to exist, the reason for adopting the particular remedy, the purpose or end sought to be attained, are all relevant facts. This is not because a good intention will save an otherwise objectionable regulation or the reverse, but because knowledge of

intent may help the court to interpret facts and to predict consequences.[3]

Some agreements and conduct under the antitrust laws are deemed to be per se illegal. "Per se illegal" means that if certain agreements or conduct are found to have existed, there is automatically an antitrust violation without any further review or need for a justification or an explanation. The courts justify the per se label on certain agreements or conduct by their conclusion that such restraints are so adverse to the role of free competition that they are to be deemed unreasonable whenever they are found to exist. The U.S. Supreme Court has explained the per se rule as follows:

> There are certain agreements or practices which because of their pernicious effect on competition and lack of any redeeming virtue are conclusively presumed to be unreasonable and therefore illegal without elaborate inquiry as to the precise harm they have caused or the business excuse for their use. . . .[4]

For example, horizontal agreements to set prices are per se illegal. Therefore, the question is not whether an agreement to fix prices by certain competitors unreasonably restrains trade, but whether the conduct or the agreement existed at all. If it did, then it is automatically illegal and the participants have violated the antitrust laws and are subject to the consequences thereof. The court will not permit any evidence on whether it was unreasonable and will not consider the question as to whether there might, in fact, be some benefit to consumers by the agreement.

For example, an agreement among competitors to set the maximum price at which to sell their products is per se illegal as price fixing, yet one might argue that it would be beneficial to the purchasers because it would put a ceiling on the price at which that product was sold. The U.S. Supreme Court, however, has determined that any agreement which in any manner affects the pricing mechanism and chills the vigor of price competition is per se illegal as price fixing. Therefore, the agreement to set a ceiling price is per se illegal.

Agreements and conduct that are considered per se illegal today, in addition to horizontal price fixing, are the following: horizontal allocation of customers, territories, or products; horizontal group boycott (concerted refusal to deal); tying arrangements; vertical price fixing (resale price maintenance); and, in many situations, vertical refusals to deal (vertical boycott) and reciprocity agreements. It is important that you learn to identify those areas of possible concern and to consult your company's attorney to help you determine whether a particular conduct or agreement might be considered per se illegal or might be suspect under a rule-of-reason test.

### Agreement (contract, combination, conspiracy)

What is an "agreement" under the antitrust laws? The Sherman, Clayton, and FTC Acts each cover certain agreements and, to some extent, the same type of agreement. The Sherman Act uses the terms "contract," "combination," and "conspiracy." For purposes of a basic antitrust understanding, those terms are synonymous with the term "agreement." The application of the law would generally be the same in each situation. In fact, the courts themselves sometimes interchange the use of the words.

The term "agreement" has a much broader definition than one might expect. It covers the obvious type of agreement, that is, a written contract between two or more parties. However, it also includes oral agreements, express or implied agreements, gentlemen's agreements, tacit understandings, and agreements evidenced by conduct rather than by words.

Thus it is extremely important to realize that your conduct may be sufficient evidence to show an "agreement" even without any evidence that even one word was spoken between the parties concerning any such "agreement." The jury or judge is permitted to find an agreement from the conduct of the parties.

The mere fact that the government or a private plaintiff cannot present direct evidence that there was an oral or written understanding among the defendants will not necessarily prevent the case from going to the judge or jury for a factual determination. The government or private plaintiff can introduce circumstantial evidence to indicate the existence of an agreement, even a tacit understanding.

### Prima facie case

The federal antitrust laws provide that if the United States brings a criminal or civil suit charging a violation of the federal antitrust laws and the defendants are found to have violated those laws, any private plaintiff can use that finding as prima facie evidence of an antitrust violation against the defendants. "Prima facie" means the plaintiff need not submit any proof of violation and the burden is on the defendant to either disprove the violation or provide certain defenses. The defendants have the opportunity to introduce evidence contra to the prima facie finding of violation. That is usually extremely difficult after an earlier finding of a violation in a government enforcement case. Therefore, generally the private suit will concentrate on proving, or disproving, damages suffered by the private plaintiff.

Consequently, the rule of prima facie evidence is often a factor in whether to litigate the antitrust charges, enter a nolo contendere (no-contest) plea in a criminal case, or enter a consent judgment in a government civil action. It is a factor because the rule of prima facie evidence does not apply to a nolo contendere plea or to a consent judgment, since there has been no trial and thus no factual finding of guilt. That is, for purposes of the plea (and for prima facie purposes) the defendant is neither admitting nor denying the facts—he is simply not contesting the charges. However, a plea of guilty in a criminal antitrust case does lead to prima facie evidence of that violation, since it is an admission of guilt—an admission that the charges are true.

As a defendant in a criminal case, your company would need to consider a nolo contendere plea and discuss the plea with its attorney. There are many factors to consider, and the finding of prima facie liability under the antitrust laws is only one, albeit a very important one, of them. In addition, some

courts will not accept a nolo contendere plea, and often the
Antitrust Division of the Department of Justice will oppose it.

A consent decree is an agreement between the government and a defendant to settle the civil action. It is generally a
written court order which contains neither an admission nor a
denial of guilt. Instead, it is a compromise resolution of the
civil matter which has been brought by either the Antitrust
Division of the Department of Justice or the Federal Trade
Commission. It also would not be prima facie evidence against
the defendant in a later private suit.

The rule of prima facie evidence of the antitrust violation applies only to enforcement actions (criminal and civil
actions) brought by the government. It does not apply to antitrust suits by the United States in which the United States is
seeking damages it allegedly suffered as a result of an antitrust
violation, as by the purchase of goods that were sold at a fixed
price. In such a situation the action is not an enforcement one;
it is an action to collect damages.

If your company may have been damaged by conduct
being prosecuted by the United States either criminally or civilly, then any verdict in favor of the government (or a plea of
guilty) will create a case of prima facie violation against the
defendants. With it your company, if you can prove recoverable damages suffered directly as a result of the conduct
charged, can recover treble damages. Naturally, the defendant
will have an opportunity to present evidence contra to the
prima facie finding of violation or in support of any other defense that might be available to it.

### Interstate commerce requirement

The federal statutes cover only anticompetitive conduct that is
either "in interstate commerce" or that substantially "affects
interstate commerce." The restriction is based on the constitutional provision that Congress can regulate only interstate
commerce and can not regulate intrastate commerce. However,
the courts have given the phrase "affects interstate commerce"
the broadest interpretation that is constitutionally permissible.[5]

The court will look at the facts in the particular case.

When it looks at conduct "in interstate commerce," the question is whether the conduct itself is in interstate commerce or "in the flow of interstate commerce." Thus, for example, if the price of widgets is fixed and the conspirators sell widgets throughout the country, then the widgets will be considered in interstate commerce or in the flow of interstate commerce.

The phrase "affects interstate commerce" applies more broadly. Even if the conduct in question is local or the product covered by the conduct is sold intrastate, it will, if it has a substantial effect in some way on interstate commerce, be covered by the federal antitrust laws. For example, the U.S. Supreme Court reviewed a situation in which a local bar association had a fee schedule for title examinations by its local attorneys. The professional service (the trade or commerce) was not in interstate commerce, but the Court held that it had a substantial effect upon interstate commerce because a substantial amount of the purchase money came from out-of-state lenders under federal mortgage insurance programs.[6]

Under the Sherman and FTC Acts either interstate commerce test can be used. The Clayton and the Robinson-Patman Acts cover only conduct "in interstate commerce," and they therefore have the more restrictive interstate commerce requirement to meet. However, if the conduct or agreement is also covered by the Sherman Act and/or the FTC Act (and often two statutes will overlap somewhat), then the test of "affects interstate commerce" can be used and the conduct or agreement can be challenged under the appropriate statute, the Sherman Act or the FTC Act.

### Intracorporate and parent-subsidiary conduct

Much of the conduct covered by the federal statutes requires that two or more persons be involved in order to be a conspiracy or an agreement. Generally, the courts have held that intracompany activity is not considered to be between two or more persons and therefore is not an agreement or conspiracy. For example, an agreement between two or more employees of the same company that the company should charge $x$ dollars per unit for its products is not price fixing.

Likewise, any agreement between unincorporated divisions of the same company is usually considered intracorporate. However, there may be situations in which the two divisions may be considered separate and therefore two parties to an agreement or conspiracy. If, for example, the two divisions formerly were separate competing corporations and have since been purchased by a parent and restructured as unincorporated divisions of the parent, with continuing separate officers and employees and a continuation to compete with different brand names, then any agreement on prices would certainly be suspect.

The more typical problem occurs between a parent and its subsidiary or a partly owned affiliated company. In those situations the court will often treat each entity as a separate party for purposes of an agreement or conspiracy and common ownership will not be the deciding factor. For example, if the owner of a cab manufacturer acquired several large cab companies in different parts of the country and entered into contracts for the sale of new cabs to those companies, the agreements would, under the antitrust laws, be deemed between two or more persons even though the persons were parent and subsidiaries or were affiliated in some other way.[7] If the agreements substantially limited competition by eliminating the manufacturer's competitors from selling cabs to the cab companies, they could be found to violate the antitrust laws.

Use of a selling agent may or may not make that selling agent part of your own corporate structure. If the selling agent is an agent for your company only, then he most likely will be considered acting on behalf of your corporation and any conduct involving the agent and your employees will be considered intracorporate. But when the selling agent represents competitors selling similar products, any agreement or understanding reached between your employees and the agent as to prices or other agreements or conduct that might be considered anticompetitive may be found to really be an agreement with the competitors represented by the selling agent. That is because the selling agent may really be a vehicle for illegal communication between your employees and the other competitors.

## Conscious parallelism

"Conscious parallelism" means conduct by various competitors that is very similar or identical and which is known by the other competitors. This type of conduct may be used as circumstantial evidence of an agreement or conspiracy.[8] Whether the conduct in question is, in and of itself, sufficient to have the judge or jury find an agreement or conspiracy depends upon the amount of such conduct, the logical implications as to who benefits from the conduct, whether the conduct is likely to have occurred without an agreement, and whether there are other logical and sound business reasons for the conduct by each of, or at least most of, the defendants. The conduct may include, for example, similar or identical price announcements, credit terms or contract terms, follow-the-leader price announcements, or identical shifts within the same period of time in the method of pricing or in the pricing formula used.

It is often said that, to show a violation by using conscious parallelism conduct, one needs the consciously parallel conduct plus evidence of something more (that is, "conscious parallelism plus").[9] What that plus is no one can really say; it will depend upon the facts in the particular case. For example, the plus may be evidence that such conduct would be detrimental to one defendant, unless performed with some understanding that all the defendants would take similar action. An example is a discontinuance of discounts, which would cause a loss of business unless all in the particular industry took the same action.

This evidence would permit the question of whether there is an implied or express agreement among the defendants to go to the trier of fact—the judge or jury. It does not say that there is or is not an agreement; the trier of fact will determine that. A defendant can, of course, introduce evidence that its conduct was the result of independent judgment and was a logical means of carrying out a business decision.

Parallel conduct may also be used to attempt to show that an implied agreement is reached solely through signals given by the conduct of competitors. For example, if for many years an industry has consistently followed a pattern of pre-printing retail prices on its product and the retailers have generally been reselling at the preprinted price without many deviations, that may be sufficient to go to the judge or jury for consideration and for a possible finding of an implied agreement implemented solely by conduct to fix the resale price of the product.

The important point is that parallel conduct, including follow-the-leader activity and advance announcements to the public (and therefore to your competitors) when there is no real need, may invite questions and an investigation of your company's activities. There is no requirement that a plaintiff, whether it be the government or a private party, show direct evidence of an agreement. The agreement can be implied.

## REFERENCES

1. *Goldfarb v. Virginia State Bar,* 421 U.S. 773, 787 n. 17 (1975).
2. *United States v. Sealy, Inc.,* 388 U.S. 350 (1967).
3. *Chicago Board of Trade v. United States,* 246 U.S. 231, 238(1918).
4. *Northern Pacific Ry. v. United States,* 356 U.S. 1, 5(1958).
5. *Goldfarb v. Virginia State Bar Assn.,* 421 U.S. 772(1975).
6. Ibid.
7. *United States v. Yellow Cab Co.,* 332 U.S. 218(1947).
8. *Interstate Circuit, Inc. v. United States,* 306 U.S. 208(1939).
9. *Theatre Enterprises, Inc. v. Paramount Film Distributing Corp.,* 346 U.S. 537(1954).

# 4

# Conduct involving your competitors

## Communications with competitors

In general, your company's goal is to make a profit. To make a profit and to compete effectively, you need to know as much about your competitors and their pricing, marketing, and selling efforts as possible. Our entire free enterprise system is built upon the philosophy that competition is to be encouraged and that the objective operation of the marketplace is the best means of keeping prices as low as practical and quality as high as demanded.

Any interference with that competitive system through some form of subjective manipulation by businesses is considered suspect. Therefore, in attempting to make a profit and to compete effectively, businesses must comply with the antitrust laws, since the basic purpose of those laws is to provide the means whereby the objective test of competition in the marketplace can occur.

One means of tampering with the objective process is for competitors to agree on some form of joint manipulation of their involvement in the competitive marketplace. Because of the vast amount of conduct among competitors that has been reviewed and often found to be anticompetitive, any joint activities among, or joint gathering of, competitors may be viewed with suspicion by a government enforcement agency and by potential private plaintiffs. Formal joint endeavors such as trade and professional associations, use of joint selling agents, use of joint purchasing agents, joint research projects and other joint ventures among competitors need to be analyzed and watched for potential antitrust problems.

But first let us look at the less formal or structured meetings or other forms of communication among competitors. Your company's contacts with your competitors through their officers, employees, agents, and representatives can give rise to suspicions of anticompetitive behavior. Such contacts can also give rise tó evidence of the *opportunity* to communicate with your competitors and possibly serve as circumstantial evidence of an anticompetitive agreement with your competitors. Therefore, innocent conduct which involves some form of joint communication between your company and your competitors can be a factor that later brings unforetold grief and expense to you and your company.

Often one aspect of an antitrust case, whether it be brought by the government or by private parties, is to show the various times when the defendant competitors met or communicated for some reason. The purpose is to show the judge or jury that the defendants had opportunities to communicate among themselves regarding the alleged anticompetitive activity. Naturally, more than merely showing opportunity is necessary to prove an antitrust case, but a showing of opportunity is circumstantial evidence that may be persuasive to the trier of fact.

Therefore, you and your company need to be careful as to when, how, and about what you meet or communicate with your competitors. In addition, conduct under review by a government enforcement agency (such as identical price announcements) plus evidence of some form of communication or meeting among the same competitors might trigger a more extensive investigation of your company and your competitors. Perfectly innocent golf outings, social gatherings, trade or professional association meetings, and telephone calls can be seen by an outside viewer as potential evidence of possible anticompetitive conduct.

*Remember, no one, other than those actually communicating, knows exactly what was discussed.* Therefore, what may be innocent communications among employees of competitors may look extremely suspect when viewed as part of a total picture of conduct by someone on the outside, such as a government enforcement agency.

The point is to be careful when, how, and about what you communicate with your competitors. When possible, have someone else present to assure that there is a witness who can confirm the innocence of the meeting. Avoid unnecessary meetings, and watch how you word written communications, including internal correspondence, when you refer to competitors. Try not to communicate with competitors prior to making a price move or making a market condition change.

### Informal communications

Naturally, there are many legitimate reasons for communicating with a competitor. You may, for example, want to purchase needed raw materials which a competitor is willing to sell to your company or discuss safety precautions regarding similar hazardous production methods. There are also many innocent social reasons why two employees of competitors might communicate or meet. However, the fact remains that what is totally legitimate and innocent can still be viewed as suspect by outsiders—those, including judge or jury, who have no actual knowledge of what actually transpired. Such circumstantial evidence of competitor communication can also be implied. (See Conscious Parallelism, above.) Because of this almost inborn suspicion, you and your company need to be cautious about such communications.

### Trade and professional associations

Trade and professional associations perform many valuable services for both the industry served and the general public; examples are the exchange of information relative to safety within the industry and upgrading the health and safety conditions of the industry's employees. However, because they are by definition groups of competitors, trade and professional associations are often looked at very closely by government antitrust enforcement agencies.

That is not to say you should not participate; it is to say you should be very careful when and under what circumstances you do participate. Whenever possible, and often it will not be practical, you should have your attorney present. That is especially true if you feel that you will be at a meeting at which some pricing discussions (or other suspect discussion) might arise or which has the potential to raise such discussions.

You may find it necessary to walk out of a meeting which includes some of your competitors when the discussion turns to prices or other suspect antitrust areas, as it might at a trade association committee meeting. Make your departure known, for the record, so that witnesses could testify that you left and did not participate in the discussions. That is not often easy to do, but you must consider the possible consequences if you don't. Advise all subordinates to be as cautious as you are in dealing with competitors through trade associations.

Your company and you personally should assess to which organizations various employees, including yourself, should belong, how helpful the organizations are, and whether the officers of the organizations are conscious of the antitrust risks and insist on avoiding any potentially suspect antitrust areas. Many trade associations have legal counsel who is very conversant in the antitrust laws and who attends every meeting. Some members will have their own legal counsel at such meetings to review proposals of the association before any vote is taken or proposal confirmed. Consider taking that course. If your company is small and it does not have its own in-house legal counsel or can not afford the expense of having outside counsel attend, then you need to be continuously conscious of your company's participation in such events.

Many trade associations are helpful to their members and to the public in general. They are aware of the antitrust laws; they take all necessary precautions not to raise any sensitive subjects at meetings or in the committees; and they do not take any action that might raise antitrust questions, such as setting up product standards for the industry, without first obtaining legal advice. Many trade associations during their meetings, including their committee meetings, will have someone read a statement into the record as to the sole purpose of the meeting. The presiding officer will then make sure that the meeting does not stray into any other discussion area.

## Use of joint agents

Having a selling or purchasing agent in common with a competitor can involve potential problems if that agent is acting on your behalf and also on behalf of your competitor. Use of such an agent may raise questions relating to whether joint use of an agent is a way to determine what price each competitor should charge (that is, price fixing), to divide up the market either geographically or by customers, or to institute a group boycott of certain sellers of products that your company buys.

Obviously, a joint purchasing or selling agent will be receiving information from competitors on the price that each of the competitors wishes to charge for its product. The agent is thus in a position to transmit that information to the other competitors and to discuss with them the market and the price to charge. With the same ease, the agent could sell the product of each competitor in a different geographical area to avoid competition or to different types of customers.

Naturally, there needs to be some form of agreement among the corporations (no matter how informal) to have a violation involving the use of a joint agent. Such an activity would certainly be very suspect, however, and it could, in fact, lead to a finding of a violation. Therefore, you need to be extremely cautious. Don't let the agent determine your prices. Obtain your information on the market from outside sources (your customers, independent market reports, your own surveys, and observations) but not by talking to your competitors or, as far as possible, solely from the agent.

Have a requirement that the agent is not to pass any pricing or market information about your company along to any of its other customers. Make sure the agent is attempting, in good faith, to sell your product in all geographic areas that are possible or practical and to all types of customers possible or practical. A requirement that the agent represent you exclusively is OK, and in fact preferable, as long as it does not create anticompetitive problems. (See Exclusive Distributorship, Chapter 10.)

### Joint research projects

Research projects carried out with any of your competitors need to be carefully analyzed from an antitrust standpoint. There is nothing per se illegal about them. However, they can not be used as a means of transmitting among competitors information that violates the antitrust laws, such as agreeing on resale prices of any products of the research effort. They can not eliminate any significant competition between you and the participating competitors.

If a project needs the combined financial or technical resources or there is significant competition from others, then it is less likely the joint project will be found violative of the antitrust laws. The test is whether any joint research agreement or any of the related provisions of the agreement unreasonably restrain trade. In other words, a court would balance the pro-competitive aspects of the joint research effort with any anti-competitive aspects and determine whether, as a whole, the project unreasonably restrains trade.

For example, joint research projects often include agreements not to share the joint research with others. If such research results are invaluable to the industry, as by making older processes or products obsolete, then the question that arises is whether the results must be shared. If the new process or product is necessary in order for a company to continue to compete effectively or for a new company to enter the market, then it may raise the antitrust question of whether a refusal to share the results is an unreasonable restraint and therefore whether that information need be shared. Naturally, if a patented process or product is involved, then the restraint in question arises out of the use of a patent. The discussion in Chapter 9 on the application of the antitrust laws to arrangements involving patents would then apply to an analysis of the situation.

If the research is developed by one company, then, unless some unique situation arises, it generally need not be shared. But the problem does arise when research is shared by at least two competitors who agree not to share the results with other competitors, and the likely result of that agreement is to drive the other competitors out of business.

When joint research is of such magnitude that it could be managed by any one of the joint participants, the question that arises is the real reason for the joint research. Is it to withhold the development from others and thereby lessen competition? If each developed the research separately, competition would originally be increased. In addition, any agreement among the researchers to withhold their separate research results from competitors would most likely be found to violate the antitrust laws.

One way to avoid possible antitrust implications in joint research projects is to permit any competitor to license the processes or the manufacturing technology at a reasonable fee. "Reasonable" generally means a fair and reasonable return to you for the risks involved in the joint research and an amount that would not place certain smaller competitors at such a disadvantage that they could not participate in the licensing program.

### Other joint ventures with competitors

In addition to research projects, competitors may have occasion to consider other joint ventures. Obviously, any joint effort by competitors will invite close scrutiny by government antitrust enforcement agencies merely because it is such an effort.

An acceptable joint effort may be to form an entity to provide better service to the group itself, such as a trade association, a news-gathering service for a group of newspapers, or an agency to ease the import or export of certain products. The joint effort may be directed toward entering a new, but related, product or geographic market, and each participant may contribute certain expertise or necessities to the joint effort. But such joint efforts as the above do invite review as potential group refusals to deal or, in the case of market extension, as raising possible merger questions.

What you need to remember is that any potential joint effort involving your company and any of its competitors should be reviewed closely before your company enters into the arrangement.

## Problems to watch for when involved with competitors

### Agreements involving prices—price fixing

Price fixing is probably the one antitrust violation that everyone feels he understands. It is still the number one concern of the antitrust enforcement agencies, and it is the one violation that frequently invites criminal sanctions against the corporation and any individual involved. It is important, however, to realize that the term "price fixing" and the probable criminal sanctions that normally attach to the act imply a much broader range of activity than one would expect. The United States Supreme Court has defined price fixing in many cases, and one of the more famous definitions is this:

> Any combination which tampers with price structures is engaged in an unlawful activity. Even though the members of the price-fixing group were in no position to control the market, to the extent that they raised, lowered or stabilized prices, they would be directly interfering with the free play of market forces. The Act places all such schemes beyond the pale and protects that vital part of our economy against any degree of interference. Congress has not left with us the determination of whether or not particular price-fixing schemes are wise or unwise, healthy or destructive. It has not permitted the age-old cry of ruinous competition and competitive evils to be a defense to price-fixing conspiracies. It has no more allowed genuine or fancy competitive abuses as a legal

justification for such schemes than it has the good intentions of the members of the combination. . . .

Under the Sherman Act a combination formed for the purpose and with the effect of raising, depressing, fixing, pegging, or stabilizing the price of a commodity in interstate or foreign commerce is illegal *per se*.[1]

Reread the above excerpt carefully. As you can see, the implication is that a lot of conduct could be included—much more than just the stereotype of the smoke-filled room in which various competitors meet to discuss and agree on a price list to follow. It can and does include much more. The antitrust laws under the terminology of price fixing prohibit an express agreement among competitors to charge a specified price for a particular product. Thus any agreement with any of your competitors to set the price at which each of you sells a particular product is an antitrust violation.

Other agreements among competitors that relate to prices, that are generally illegal, and that are called price fixing include those listed below. Please bear in mind that, in order to prove a price-fixing agreement, it is not necessary to show that there is an agreement among all of the competitors. The following agreements among competitors would be deemed illegal:

On the minimum price to be charged.
On the maximum price to be charged.
On the base price to be used.
On the price at which negotiations with potential purchasers are to start.
On price lists from which actual prices are discounted.
On withholding a portion of the supply.
On setting production quotas.
On establishing a basing point system for determining delivered prices.
To rig bids.
To discontinue a product.
To set certain specifications and standards (in some cir-

cumstances these may be all right; see discussion of use of standards requirements and certificates of approval in this chapter).

To set discounts, allowances, or rebates.

To eliminate discounts, allowances, or rebates.

To establish use of standard cost.

To establish a minimum, maximum, or set markup.

To establish uniform trade-in allowances.

To establish uniform commission rates or schedules.

To eliminate trade-in allowances.

To establish uniform fee schedules.

To depress prices at which to buy certain raw materials.

To purchase raw materials only at fixed prices or at not more than set maximum prices.

To establish other uniform terms or conditions of the sale.

To buy up excess quantities of production and hold them off the market.

To limit price advertisement.

To refrain from providing bonuses or trading stamps.

It is therefore important to recognize the widespread application of the term "price fixing" and the consequences of participation or even any appearance of participation in such an agreement. That means you and your company need to be sensitive to any contact with competitors.

There are many do's and don'ts in the price-fixing area. They are not necessarily to be interpreted as implying that such conduct is illegal, but the conduct can be evidence of or an implication of your company's participation in some form of agreement to "raise, depress, fix, peg, or stabilize prices." Some of the do's and don'ts are:

• Don't agree upon or even discuss with any of your competitors any of the above listed matters.

• Don't discuss or exchange past, present, or future information relating to market shares, costs, prices, production figures, discounts, rebates, allowances, or other terms of sale with any of your competitors. Even loose talk can become very expensive talk for your company if it is construed as evidence of a form of a price-fixing agreement.

• Don't discuss your pricing policies, methods, or formulas with any competitor.

• Avoid unnecessary contacts with your competitors' representatives.

• Be careful where and how you obtain information on your competitors' prices; obtain the pricing information from customers or independent third parties and not from your competitors.

• Be careful not to always follow the leader in determining your prices, especially when a pattern of price determination has developed in your industry such that it is predictable who will lead, how soon others will follow, by what percent, and so on.

• Determine which trade and professional associations and which of their meetings are necessary and beneficial from a business standpoint, and attend only those that are necessary and beneficial.

• Send to a trade association meeting only employees who will actually benefit.

• Do not exchange price lists with or send out price lists to competitors.

• If you receive a competitor's price list, have your attorney ask that the action stop immediately.

• When it is necessary to talk to competitors from a legitimate business standpoint, make it a point, when possible, to talk to someone who does not have pricing authority. Alternatively, have one of your employees who does not have pricing authority contact the competitor.

• Do not permit phone calls from an employee who has pricing authority to a competitor's employee who has pricing authority unless the call is absolutely necessary and has a legitimate business purpose.

• Be careful of providing to various organizations statistical data that relate to past, present, or future prices, market shares, costs, production figures, discounts, rebates, allowances, or other terms of sale without first consulting your attorney.

• Be careful of using joint sales or purchasing agents. If they are used, be careful of giving them authority related to pricing and other terms and conditions of the sale or purchase and where and to whom to sell or from whom to buy.

• Document your price increases (for example, show how the increase is based on increased costs and so on) and decreases (for example, show a reduction in certain costs).

• To the extent that is possible, document price increases or decreases and changes in any terms of sale as part of the normal course of business.

• To the extent that is practical, document the reasons for significant changes in production, quality, or any other significant factor in your competitive role.

• In industries in which the product is homogeneous, prices will be very similar; therefore, it is especially important to keep a record of how and when your prices were determined. The documentation will help substantiate that price moves, even though similar to others in the industry, were determined on the basis of valid business reasoning.

• Discuss with your attorney any situation you feel may cause future antitrust problems or which raises an antitrust question in your mind.

### Allocation by competitors of customers, geographic markets, or products

An agreement among competitors to divide up customers, geographic markets, or products is a per se violation. Thus any understanding among competitors as to where to compete or not to compete, with respect to geography or customers, or what product lines to produce or not to produce is illegal. That includes situations in which some compete in one area but others do not, and all agree to maintain the status quo. It includes situations in which a potential competitor agrees not to enter a particular market, possibly in exchange for certain other potential competitors not entering its market. The U.S. Supreme Court has said:

One of the classic examples of a *per se* violation . . . is an agreement between competitors at the same level of the market structure to allocate territories in order to minimize competition. Such concerted action is usually termed a "horizontal" restraint, in contradistinction to combinations of persons at different levels of the market structure, e.g., manufacturers and distributors, which are termed "vertical" restraints. This Court has reiterated time and time again that "horizontal territorial limitations . . . are naked restraints of trade with no purpose except stifling of competition." . . . Such limitations are *per se* violations of the Sherman Act.[2]

The Court has thus determined that it is not a defense to argue any justification for or public benefit from any such agreement. Therefore, you need to be careful of the following situations:

• It would be illegal for a group of firms to agree among themselves not to compete with each other with the same products and to predetermine which firm carries what product.

• The above situation would be illegal even if it were a group of small firms that determined among themselves who would sell what products in order to be able to compete against larger firms.

• It would be illegal for a group of competitors to form a buying association to increase their buying power in order to obtain products at lower cost and include an agreement that the association would have its own brand and no association member would expand into another member's territory and compete with that association's brand or a similar agreement.

• It is important to note that any division of customers, geographic markets, or products among competitors is illegal even if it is made through some form of umbrella association or company. Thus it is likely that a court would view as a horizontal agreement any agreement on division of customers, geographic markets, or products arising from a manufacturing company wholly owned by its distributors. If, for example, the distributors owned the stock of a manufacturing company (the "umbrella") and therefore, in reality, controlled the decision making, then any allocation of exclusive territories, customers, or products would most likely be viewed as an agreement among competitors (the distributors) to allocate exclusive territories and would therefore be per se illegal.

• The prohibition of a horizontal allocation of customers, territories, or products applies to agreements involving either intrabrand or interbrand products. Thus if distributors of a particular brand of product allocate territories only in regard to that brand of the product, it is per se illegal. That is true even though each distributor would still have competition from other brands of that product. There have been recent opinions that this form of horizontal division of territories should not be considered necessarily anticompetitive but should be looked at under the rule-of-reason test to determine if it is an unreasonable restraint in the particular situation in question. At present, however, it is still a per se violation.

• If a manufacturer or wholesaler is used by a group of its purchasers to allocate customers, territories, or products, such a situation will most likely be considered horizontal. That is probably true whether the purchasers pressured or threatened the manufacturer or distributor to so allocate or whether all agreed to it as "good business sense."

• A division of exclusive marketing territories by a manufacturer or distributor within which customers can resell the manufacturer's or distributor's products is a true vertical arrangement and is viewed under the rule-of-reason test. (See the discussion in Chapter 5.)

• Remember, generally, that any number of competitors can agree without the violation being any less a violation. Even the size of the competitor is irrelevant. If small firms agree to allocate the market, then the violation is per se just as an agreement among larger firms would be.

• Be careful about any implied understanding with competitors "not to rock the boat" or "not to disturb the status quo" as to other geographic or product markets, new groups of customers, or attempts to increase your "share of the market."

• An agreement to divide up among competitors the customers who require bids is another form of allocation of customers. For example, an agreement by a group of suppliers as to which supplier would be entitled to bid for which government business—even if there are other possible bidders—is per se illegal as a horizontal allocation of customers. It does not matter whether or not there was any agreement on what price would be bid by the assigned supplier.

• The same is true of any agreement to refrain from submitting price quotes to certain customers.

Therefore:

• When you are considering new markets or customers, do not discuss your prospective actions with your competitors or potential competitors. Depending upon the results of your conduct or lack of entry into the considered market, the discussion might be viewed by outside third parties, such as government antitrust enforcement agencies, as evidence of a conspiracy. In other words, if you talk to your competitors or potential competitors about entering a market, manufacturing a product you do not presently manufacture, extending your product line, or adding a new group of customers and you do not enter, only partially enter, or enter and then withdraw from such market, your company's actions may be viewed as evidence of an agreement of allocation among you and your competitors and as evidence of the consequences of that agreement even though your company's actions may be totally innocent.

• If you are considering withdrawing from a market—geographic, product, or customer—do not discuss the possibility with or survey your competitors. To do so can be misinterpreted by someone who views the activity from the outside.

• Since your company obviously needs market information when it is considering the possibility of entering into or withdrawing from a particular market, obtain the information from sources other than your competitors or potential competitors. It may be available from published market studies or surveys, government agencies, or customers. Another possibility is to have an independent market consultant determine the market information you need. If necessary, the consultant might obtain information from your competitors, accumulate it, summarize it, and provide it to you in a form such that you will not be able to determine what information came from which particular competitor. It will therefore not be any communication between your company and your competitors. That course is somewhat risky, but it is preferable to your company's dealing directly with your competitors.

• You need to be careful when using or considering the use of a selling agent also used by some of your competitors or potential competitors. To do so may be viewed, depending on other facts, as a vehicle for implementing and allocating customers, territories, or products.

• Document as a regular part of your business operations any decisions to enter into, withdraw from, or not enter into any market, whether geographic, customer, or product.

The antitrust laws require that there be an "agreement" or "conspiracy" before there is a violation for a horizontal allocation of market. That does not exclude independent action by an individual company. Your company can enter into or withdraw from any market it pleases as long as the action is not part of an agreement (with the proviso that there are no non-antitrust reasons why it can not and that such withdrawal does not create another antitrust problem such as joint boycott or an unfair method of competition under the FTC Act). Likewise, there can be several competitors withdrawing and/or entering a new market at about the same time if each makes its own independent business decision to do so. However, similar conduct or conduct that for any reason may look questionable to an outside third party may raise suspicions and cause a government investigation and/or a private or government suit. So, even though in your heart you know you are right, you must also be aware how it looks to someone who is not that familiar with your industry and your conduct.

### Boycott of competitors—concerted refusals to buy or sell

Basically, a horizontal *boycott* or *concerted refusal to deal* is an agreement among a group of competitors to deprive another competitor or other competitors, directly or indirectly, of a particular commercial relationship that is helpful in competing effectively against the competitors in the group. Such an agreement often is considered a per se violation.[3]

Here we are considering factual situations such as those listed below. We are not looking at situations in which there is a vertical refusal to deal agreement between, say, a manufacturer and a distributor whereby the manufacturer will terminate, or refuse to deal, with another distributor. These situations are discussed in Chapter 5. Likewise, an individual decision to refuse to deal with another company is not discussed here but is covered in Chapter 5.

A joint effort by a group of competitors to cause a boycott of other competitors may take various forms and be for various reasons:

• Certain competitors may jointly refuse to deal with a particular purchaser or supplier or group of purchasers or suppliers unless they "shape up" and discontinue their business relationship, or a particular phase of it, with a targeted competitor or targeted group of competitors. For example, a group of wholesalers may advise one of their suppliers that the wholesalers will not purchase from that supplier unless it ceases to supply a particular group of competitors of the wholesalers.

• A group of distributors may pressure the supplier to quit selling to another distributor—a discounter, for example.

• It may also take the form of a single firm pressuring or obtaining the acquiescence of a certain key supplier or suppliers not to sell to the firm's competitor.

• Generally, in a horizontal boycott (concerted refusal to deal) case the courts will not permit any defense based on a justification for the action. For example, a joint boycott by original dress design manufacturers to refuse to sell to any retail store that did not refrain from buying the products of certain "style pirates" is illegal, even though the action might be taken for a supposedly justifiable reason (to eliminate the companies pirating the styles of the various original designers), which might include a right of action against the pirates under other legal theories.[4]

### Improper use of standards requirements; certificates of approval by associations

A joint refusal to deal may arise when a certain "certificate of approval" is needed, helpful, or advantageous to compete in a particular industry and the awarding of that approval is by a less than totally objective test. If competitors determine which companies or products receive the certificate of approval or if competitors, in whole or in part, make up the committee that makes such a determination, the member competitors must be careful to keep the granting and denial of the approval as objective and consistent as possible.

In addition, the underlying standards themselves must be examined to make sure they include only the standards minimally necessary for that particular industry or product and do not include standards that keep out otherwise competent competitors or competitive products. For example, a standard directed at testing certain types of products, such as electrical equipment, to meet minimum safety requirements would most likely be valid if not excessively high and not applied subjectively.

### Self-regulation of industry or profession

The self-regulation of an industry or profession must be carefully policed in order to avoid allegations of illegal boycott. Generally, a boycott or the threat of a boycott, no matter of what form, cannot be used to self-regulate an industry or profession. That is especially true when the determination or application of the standards is less than totally objective and/or less than reasonable under the circumstances.[5] It may have the effect of keeping out potential competitors through unnecessarily high requirements or excessive disciplinary action and is therefore very likely to be considered anticompetitive.

Certain standards (for example, codes of ethics) for regulating an industry or profession and/or its products or services are generally acceptable as long as they are not out of line with what is reasonable for regulating for the public health or safety or other public interest and preferably are determined on an objective basis. Generally, the standards should be the minimum that is necessary and still meet the legitimate public interest to be protected.

As an employee of a competitor, be careful in participating in the setting up of standards, in enforcing industry standards, and/or licensing professional members or industry members. If there is talk about keeping a certain potential competitor or group of potential competitors out or adding new improper standards, make sure your opposition and lack of participation are well noted. That may include leaving the meeting and having your exit duly noted.

Some forms of licensing and self-regulation are valid. The limited exceptions depend upon each set of particular facts and involve situations which can be objectively justified as in the public interest. That might include some minimal self-regulation for public health or safety reasons or when there is legislative authority for self-regulation.

It is important to remember:

• There should be standards for a "certificate of approval" for products or admission into the organization only when the industry or profession is such that some self-regulation is required for public health or safety reasons or when there is legislative authority for self-regulation.

• Professions may generally have some minimum form of self-regulation either by statutory authority or by self-imposition.

• Only standards of admission into an industry or standards for a "certificate of approval" that are objective and reasonable should be used.

• Codes of ethics or codes of conduct generally cannot contain anticompetitive provisions unless there is some overriding public interest reason for them. For example, a ban on advertising by attorneys[6] and a ban prohibiting the submission of competitive bids by engineers prior to their initial employment, even though allegedly to protect the public from selecting an engineer on a basis other than merit,[7] have been held illegal.

An antitrust action alleging a boycott or a concerted refusal to deal might include each participant in the alleged conspiracy. That might mean each participant in the association or on the licensing board, commission, standards committee, or any other regulatory body. For example, the suit might include, as a defendant, each member of the standards committee, the admissions committee, and/or the entire association.

Some possible means to avoid potential antitrust problems in this area include:

• Make membership available to all members of the industry or profession, especially when membership is helpful or necessary to compete effectively.

• Provide an executive director who has no direct connection with the industry or profession to review the various standards and determine that they are objective and that they are applied objectively.

• Standards should be published and available to all members and potential members.

• To the extent that is practical, share the benefits, such as industrywide research and industry promotional advertising, within the industry.

• Membership or a certificate of approval should be denied only on objective grounds and preferably by other than member competitors, as by review of the executive director.

• Any ban against price cutters or discounters or a ban on price advertising or entering new product lines would generally be a violation of the antitrust laws and should therefore be eliminated.

• Members on standards committees, admission committees, and similar groups should be noncompetitors to the extent possible.

• Justification based on social or moral reasons or the elimination of undesirable industry or profession practices often will not be valid defenses.

• One may need procedural safeguards for someone who may be terminated as a member, such as notice of a complaint or possible dismissal and a hearing to counter any question of reasonableness. A failure to have procedural safeguards may be sufficient to show that a rule is unreasonable and therefore anticompetitive.

• Notice and hearing for review of any refusal to certify a business' product is suggested.[8]

• Trade associations also need to be careful. For example, a trade association of local hotels was formed to attract convention business to a particular city. Each supplier was required to pay a fee to the association, and any supplier that did not was not to be used by any member hotel. The association was held to be engaged in an illegal boycott, per se, even though its purpose was to attract convention business. It deprived competitor suppliers of an opportunity to attempt to sell to the hotels.[9]

• In some situations, primarily when some form of association is involved, the courts will apply a rule-of-reason test to the rule, regulation, bylaw, or conduct in question if there is no evidence of any concurrent price fixing, allocation of territory, or other per se anticompetitive conduct.

• Excessive membership dues, waiting time, number of references, or research cost investment may be unlawful if it restricts smaller competitors from membership.

• It is preferable to set up a method of hearing before a certificate of approval for a product is denied. For example, a review committee of nonmembers can hear the positions of the association and the individual member seeking the certificate of approval and make a determination based on the opportunity for full presentation and with some objective standards to guide them.

• Standards helpful to the industry and to consumers are generally permissible as they relate to product standardization when the standardization does not affect competition or is only ancillary to its main legitimate purpose. Examples are sizes, weights, content weight, capacity, and related standards that help purchasers comparison-shop for products that can be interchanged. The more procompetitive, governmental (for example, environmental), and/or safety reasons to explain the standardization balanced against the anticompetitive impact, the better.

• However, certain standardization may be unlawful if it becomes so costly that some competitors cannot meet it or enter the field.

• Codes of ethics of and self-regulation by professions may be viewed somewhat more leniently than those of other businesses since the U.S. Supreme Court has indicated that self-regulation of a profession may be in the public interest.[10] However, such codes of ethics or self-regulation can not cover conduct that would be per se illegal, such as a determination of fee schedules, a ban on advertising, or a ban on submission of price quotes.*

### Use of unfair competition to eliminate a competitor

It may be a violation of the antitrust laws to use unfair means to eliminate a competitor. Such unfair means would include (1) hiring away the competitor's key employees, (2) wrongfully obtaining a "trade secret" customer list, and (3) trade disparagement.[11] Several courts have held that use of these and similar means, especially if the company using the unfair competition is a dominant company, is an antitrust violation. At least one court has described such action as a per se offense.

Other courts have held that such conduct, although it may violate other laws, did not amount to an antitrust violation. The present conflict as to whether such conduct is an antitrust violation has not been resolved by the U.S. Supreme Court. It is important that you realize that it may be construed as an antitrust violation, perhaps even a per se violation. Your company would then be subject to a treble damage judgment being awarded against it.

### REFERENCES

1. *United States v. Socony-Vacuum Oil Co.*, 310 U.S. 150, 221–23(1940).
2. *United States v. Topco Associates, Inc.*, 405 U.S. 596, 608(1972).
3. *Klor's, Inc. v. Broadway-Hale Stores*, 359 U.S. 207(1959).
4. *Fashion Originators' Guild of America, Inc. v. FTC*, 312 U.S. 457(1941).

*The FTC has issued a proposed trade regulation rule on "standards and certification" including procedures for application of standards to individual companies. The FTC states there are presently about 20,000 standards.

5. *Radiant Burners, Inc. v. Peoples Gas Light & Coke Co.*, 364 U.S. 656(1961).
6. *Bates v. State Bar of Arizona*, 433 U.S. 350(1977). Decided on First Amendment grounds that consumers have a right to know. Antitrust issues also were raised.
7. *National Society of Professional Engineers v. United States*, 435 U.S. 679(1978).
8. *Silver v. New York Stock Exchange*, 373 U.S. 341(1963).
9. *United States v. Hilton Hotels Corp.*, 467 F. 2d 1000 (9th Cir. 1972), cert. denied, sub nom. 409 U.S. 1125(1973).
10. *Goldfarb v. Virginia State Bar*, 421 U.S. 773, 787 n. 17(1975).
11. *Albert Pick-Barth Co. v. Mitchell Woodbury Corp.*, 57 F. 2d 96(1st. Cir.), cert. denied, 286 U.S. 552(1932).

# 5

# Conduct involving entities in your company's chain of distribution

As a manufacturer, supplier, distributor, franchiser, franchisee, and/or customer, your company needs to understand what it can and cannot do in dealing with your customers, franchisees, franchiser, distributors, suppliers, and/or manufacturers. That is true whether you sell a tangible or intangible product or a service. Although the basic determination of the antitrust laws is that you can deal with whom you please, in reality the exceptions to the rule are so broad and so inclusive that they practically swallow up the rule.

Quite naturally, manufacturers and producers (including franchisers) want to control the marketing of their products so that the reputation of the brand or of the manufacturer or producer itself is upheld and maximum sales are obtained. Likewise, distributors, wholesalers, jobbers, franchisees, and retailers want to be able to obtain as large a share of the market for a particular product or service as possible and at as profitable a price as possible.

How those reasonable wants are met, to what extent, and with what form of conduct is all-important. Relationships within the vertical chain of distribution are subject to the antitrust laws, and thus certain vertical arrangements and conduct may be illegal under the antitrust laws.

The other side of the coin, of course, is that your company has the right to expect certain conduct from those it deals with, and certain legal remedies have been provided under the antitrust laws if it has been damaged by illegal conduct.

## Agreement on resale prices

### Illegal agreements

You may recall the fair trade laws that were in effect in various states until several years ago. Under certain conditions, the state laws permitted a manufacturer of a branded product sold in competition with other products to set the minimum price, and in some cases the exact price, at which its product could be resold and have the retailer agree to sell at that price or not below the minimum price. Congress in 1937, and as amended in 1952, passed federal legislation to permit a state to exempt from violation of the federal antitrust laws any resale price agreement entered into in compliance with that state's fair trade law. Without the federal statutory exemption, the agreement on the resale price would have been an antitrust violation if it came within coverage of the federal statutes, that is, if it was in or affected interstate commerce. The federal antitrust laws prohibit an agreement between a supplier (manufacturer) and its customer on the price at which the customer will resell the product. The federal exemption was repealed in 1975, and today any resale price agreement within coverage of the federal antitrust statutes would be illegal per se.[1]

Thus an agreement between a seller of a product and a buyer who plans to resell that product as to what the resale price of the product shall be is per se illegal under the antitrust laws. That includes resale price agreements between a manufacturer and a distributor, a manufacturer and a wholesaler, a wholesaler and a retailer, a licensor and a licensee, or a franchiser and a franchisee.

Agreements that are illegal include those on the exact resale price to be charged, on minimum prices, on maximum prices, on amounts of discounts or rebates, or on any other aspect of the resale price or other terms of sale. That is true whether the product is resold under the manufacturer's trademark or trade name or another brand or name. It also applies to patented and unpatented products and copyrighted matter.

It is important to realize that an agreement on resale price maintenance can be illegal even though the exact price has not been agreed upon by the parties. It is also important to remember that the violation is per se, and therefore there is no question of reasonableness of the agreement or of the restraint of trade. Both are presumed unreasonable and therefore illegal if the fact of agreement can be shown.

### Unilateral action by seller to require resale price

The Colgate doctrine (so named because it was first identified in the case of *United States v. Colgate & Co.*)[2] states that if a seller acts alone, and not in concert with any other party, it can refuse to sell to anyone that will not follow its predetermined resale price for its product as long as that product is in competition with other products. In other words, a seller could set a resale price and either refuse to sell or discontinue selling to any buyer that would not follow that resale price.

However, the Colgate doctrine, although still alive, has been narrowed a great deal by the courts. If there is any evidence of any involvement of a third party, such as another seller or buyer, in implementing, policing, or coercing compliance with the resale price set by the first seller, an "agreement" will be found by the court between that first seller and any contributing seller or buyer.[3] Therefore, an illegal resale price maintenance agreement will exist.

For example, if a wholesaler uses some of its buyers to inform it of any deviation by any retailer from the resale price set by it, the arrangement most likely will be sufficient to find a resale price maintenance agreement if the wholesaler takes any action to terminate the wayward retailer or to force that retailer to comply with the predetermined price. Likewise, if the seller finds a recalcitrant buyer and gives it a "second chance," an agreement to sell at the set price most likely will be found between the seller and that buyer.

At most, the seller can announce that it will not sell to anyone, or will discontinue selling to anyone who does not sell at the set resale price. Then if a buyer violates that announcement, it must be terminated—no second chances, no use of "informers" or "policemen." In other words, as long as the conduct is one way, that is, from seller to buyer, it falls within the Colgate doctrine. As soon as there is any opportunity for the court to find any form of "agreement" with any other party, it will most likely do so. That includes an agreement involving the buyer, any other seller, or any other third party such as a joint selling agent. It also includes a situation in which the seller warns or threatens the buyer but gives the buyer a second chance to comply with the resale price schedule. Even though the buyer was coerced into following the resale price set by the seller, the court would still view the situation as an agreement for antitrust purposes.

### Use of promotions to require resale price compliance

You need to be careful about tying a promotion in with a resale price agreement. For example, a representation that your company will provide promotions only to companies that agree to pass the promotion discounts on to the customers or sell at no more than a certain ceiling price or at a minimum price or some other pricing condition may be construed as an agreement between your company and the buyer to fix the resale price or some aspect of the resale price.

### "Suggested" resale prices; preticketing

You need to be cautious about preticketing items that you sell with the "suggested" retail prices. If those prices are consistently followed by retailers, that may raise a question as to an implied agreement that retailers will resell at the preticketed prices. (The FTC has also questioned whether consistently selling items at lower than preticketed prices may not be deceptive trade practice because it leads the public to believe that it is getting a discount from a normally higher price.) In addition, if any coercion by the seller to force compliance with the suggested price is shown, then there is the possibility that a court will find an illegal resale price maintenance agreement.

### Sham use of "consignment" or "agent"

As stated above, you can deal with whom you wish. In theory, that applies to requiring that certain prices be followed in the resale of your product. There must be no agreement with anyone else regarding the prices charged by a particular distributor. Any attempt to circumvent that prohibition by calling a sale a "consignment" or a purchaser an "agent" will be unsuccessful, and the court will look at the substance rather than the form.[4]

A true consignment or agency relationship is not a sale, and you can dictate the price at which you want your own property to be sold: the sale is not a resale, but the first sale of your product. However, merely calling a transaction a "consignment" or a business relationship an "agency relationship" will not make it one if all or many of the obligations of a true sale are placed on the recipient, and it is likely to be deemed a sale by the court. For example, some indicia of a sale are who bears the risk of loss, the costs of insurance, the cost of promotions, the cost of the unsold product, and the cost of salaries and benefits.

### Rule applied to franchiser-franchisee relationship

The vertical price-fixing rules apply to the franchiser-franchisee relationships as well, and any agreement that franchisees will follow a certain resale price will be illegal per se. There are situations in which the franchiser implements certain requirements to preserve the quality of its trademark or to comply with certain state or federal regulations imposed upon the franchise arrangement. The actions are generally considered legitimate as long as they do not include a direct vertical price-fixing requirement. For example, if the franchiser has developed an image for a quality product within a certain price range, it may be able to work with a franchisee on pricing ranges and possibly even require a franchisee to price within a range consistent with the franchiser's image.

*Consult Your Attorney.* This area is fraught with pitfalls; and before you embark upon any resale price maintenance program, it would be wise to consult with your attorney. The same is true in a franchiser–franchisee arrangement involving any franchise requirements relating to the resale price to be charged by the franchisee.

## Refusing to deal with a supplier or purchaser; termination of a distributor or supplier

### Unilateral refusal to deal with a customer

Generally, as mentioned under Agreement on Resale Prices earlier in this chapter, a supplier basically has the right to select its customers as long as it does so unilaterally and customers are not excluded because of some form of understanding with a third party. The rule, however, has many limitations and potential pitfalls, both when the company attempts to unilaterally require a predetermined resale price (as previously discussed under Agreement on Resale Prices) and when it selects, renews, or terminates distributors, franchisees, or other customers. Here we will discuss the potential problems in dealing with customers, whether the customer be a distributor, franchisee, licensee, or other type of customer.

A refusal to sell to or deal with a particular customer, a refusal to renew a supply, distribution, or franchise agreement, or the termination of a distributor, franchisee, or other customer generally is not unlawful when the decision is a unilateral one by the supplier. It must not be part of any conspiracy by competitors of a particular distributor, franchisee, or other customer, part of some other form of predatory scheme by the supplier to restrain competition, or part of an attempt to monopolize. Alternative products must also be available, and there are no extenuating facts. However, since most situations in the real world contain more complex facts, it is wise to consult with your attorney before you terminate a present distributor, franchisee, or other customer or even refuse to sell to a new customer.

### Illegal refusal to deal with a customer

In determining whether a certain action taken against a customer or potential customer is in violation of the antitrust laws as an illegal refusal to deal, the courts generally look at whether the action makes business sense and is not contrary to the supplier's economic interest. Further, the courts review any motivation present that would prompt the supplier to take such action, assuming there is no direct evidence of an illegal agreement to refuse to deal.

The courts are unclear as to whether an agreement on a vertical refusal to deal is per se illegal or is to be reviewed under the rule-of-reason test. However, it should be your guide that any anticompetitive purpose or effect of such agreement or conspiracy most likely will result in the court finding a violation. A valid business reason for a unilateral refusal to deal is the best rationale for the activity. Once a third party becomes involved, the risks of a possible antitrust violation are increased.

Even unilateral action may be deemed in violation of section 5 of the FTC Act if it is found to be an unfair method of competition. Under such circumstances the FTC may bring an action enjoining you from such activity. The fact that only one distributor, franchisee, or other customer is excluded is irrelevant. Nor is the mere fact that there may be many other distributors of that same product within a particular market area a defense to an anticompetitive refusal to deal with that one distributor.[5]

Decisions to terminate or refuse to deal with a particular distributor, franchisee, or other customer should be documented at the time of the decision. The business reasons for the actions should be noted. You may also consider whether you want to state those business reasons to the customer in writing. In some cases, doing so may prevent a lawsuit.

Your company can distribute its own products without violating the antitrust laws as long as there is no evidence of any anticompetitive purpose in doing so or evidence of an attempt to monopolize. You need to be extra careful of how you handle independent distributors, franchisees, or other customers if you, as a supplier, also have your own competing distribution system. A disgruntled customer may charge a conspiracy between the supplier and its subsidiary distributor to attempt to monopolize or to eliminate the others as competitors.

### Potential involvement in conspiracy as customer

Since distributors, franchisees, and other customers can become involved as parties to a vertical conspiracy of refusing to deal, your company, as a customer, needs to be sensitive to any potential involvement. That includes any understanding between your company and a supplier regarding the termination of one of the supplier's distributors, franchisees, or other customers (your competitors). Likewise, it can include involvement in some other form of vertical refusal to deal with a customer by one of your suppliers.

You naturally will also want to be sensitive to being used as a vehicle in effectuating a horizontal refusal to deal. (See the discussion of joint efforts by competitors to boycott in Chapter 4.)

It is important to realize that if, as a competitor of a distributor, your company becomes part of an agreement with its supplier to refuse to deal with that distributor, the agreement may be viewed as a horizontal refusal to deal. That, without question, is considered per se illegal, and there would be no valid business justification for the agreement.

### Valid reasons for termination or refusal to deal

The following situations generally have been held to be valid business reasons for refusing to deal with or terminating a distributor, franchisee, or other customer. (It is assumed there are no extenuating facts and it is recommended that you have a prior consultation with your attorney.)

Termination because of a distributor or franchisee's poor performance.

Termination for failure to maintain the supplier's image.

Termination pursuant to a provision permitting either party at any time to terminate without cause.

Termination to replace one exclusive distributor with another, possibly even at the suggestion of the other.

Refusal to sell your product to other than franchised dealers.

Termination or refusal to sell because of poor credit or other financial difficulties of the distributor.

Termination because of a change in ownership and/or management of the distributor or franchisee.

Termination in order to obtain a statewide distributor.

Termination or refusal to deal because you desire better equipped and more aggressive distributors or franchisees.

Termination for failure to effectively promote and develop sales for the suppliers' products.

Termination of independent distributors or franchisees and substitution of your own internal distribution system in order to provide more efficient delivery or lower costs and/or to gain control over your sales force.

Termination for handling competing lines.

There may be other state or federal statutes that might prevent termination of or refusal to renew a distributor or franchisee. Examples are state franchise statutes or statutes governing particular industries such as the automobile and petroleum industries. There may also be contractual provisions prohibiting termination.

### Agreement to divide up the market by geographic, product, or customer allocation

If you have a distribution system or franchise system, you may wish to assign territories to particular franchisees or distributors. You may even want a prohibition against the franchisee or distributor entering into another franchisee's or distributor's territory. You may want to put some form of restriction on the products or on the customers to whom the distributors or franchisees can sell.

Any restriction on a franchisee or distributor as to the territory in which it can sell or generally compete, the products it can sell, or the customers to which it can sell is subject to antitrust review. Each of the restrictions puts some limitation on the distributor's or franchisee's ability to compete on an intrabrand basis (that is, with other distributors or franchisees of the same brand of the product) and possibly also on its ability to compete on an interbrand basis, as by limiting the geographic scope of its sphere of competition. A restriction would be reviewed under a rule-of-reason test, and a determination as to whether it was anticompetitive or procompetitive would be made. Since such a restriction would most likely lessen any intrabrand competition, a court would primarily look at whether it was offset by promotion of interbrand competition.

Basically, then, a situation involving any such restriction in the vertical chain of distribution would come under the rule-of-reason test. If an individual distributor or franchisee puts pressure on the supplier or franchiser to allocate the market among the distributors or franchisees, the arrangement is a vertical one between the supplier-distributor or franchiser-franchisee and comes under the rule-of-reason test. However, if interbrand competition is being allocated among territories, products, or customers, then the arrangement becomes a horizontal allocation of markets and is per se illegal. The reason it is horizontal is that it really is an agreement among competitors to allocate the markets. That may also be true in a situation in which franchisees or distributors put pressure on the supplier or franchiser to allocate markets among them. If the effort is a group one, then again it is a matter of competitors attempting to divide up the market among themselves through use of the supplier or franchiser.

It is important to make the distinction between vertical and horizontal allocation. A horizontal allocation of markets by competitors is per se illegal, whereas a vertical arrangement involving a supplier or franchiser allocating markets among its distributors or franchisees is valid unless the arrangement unreasonably restrains trade (the rule-of-reason test).

Thus if a supplier wishes to allocate territories within which or determine the location from which its distributors or other customers can resell the particular products, the validity of that agreement under the antitrust laws will be determined under the rule-of-reason test. Again it is the basic balancing of the procompetitive aspects versus the anticompetitive aspects of the restrictions. For example, in the case of *Continental T.V. Inc. v. GTE Sylvania, Inc.*[6] (which was the case in which the U.S. Supreme Court determined that the rule-of-reason test, and not the per se illegality standard, should apply to vertical allocation of markets) GTE Sylvania ultimately was able to convince the court that its restrictions on the locations from which Sylvania television sets could be distributed was procompetitive rather than anticompetitive. Sylvania had an extremely small percentage of the market, and the territory restriction permitted a distributor to expend time and money promoting the Sylvania products without being concerned about intrabrand competition within its territory. Interbrand competition was thereby enhanced. Sylvania was also able to show that its share of the market increased from 1 to 3 percent as a result of the exclusive territories.

The following are some factors the courts would consider in determining whether territory restrictions are unreasonable:

> How strong is the interbrand competition?
> How large a percent of the interbrand market does the supplier have?
> Is the supplier a relatively new competitor in the market?
> Is the supplier a failing company in the market?
> Was the intrabrand competition that was eliminated actually present or only potential?
> Are the restrictions necessary to obtain aggressively competitive distributors or franchisees?
> The amount of commitment in terms of dollars and effort needed from the distributors or franchisees.

Evidence that interbrand competition has been promoted.

The extent to which interbrand competition has been enhanced.

Are there less restrictive means to accomplish the same result?

Are the restrictions tied to illegal conduct such as vertical fixing of resale price to be charged by the distributor or franchisee?

The exclusive distributor arrangement discussed under "Refusing to Deal with a Supplier or Purchaser; Termination of a Distributor or Supplier" in this chapter goes hand in glove with the conduct of vertical allocation of territories, since exclusive distributorships must be considered under such tests. Thus the fact that you have an exclusive dealership arrangement means that you need look at both the refusal to deal limitations and the market allocation limitations under the antitrust laws. In addition, exclusive distributor arrangements would be subject to review as an exclusive dealing arrangement. See the discussion on exclusive dealing arrangements elsewhere in this chapter.

### Other non-price restrictions placed on a distributor or franchisee

A requirement that a distributor have an "area of primary responsibility" basically means that the distributor has a geographic area in which it is primarily responsible and in which it is to use its primary efforts to promote and sell the products. An area of primary responsibility is easier to justify under a rule-of-reason test than a strict allocation of territories would be. There is no requirement that the distributor not sell outside its area of primary responsibility; instead, there is a requirement that its efforts be concentrated in that area to encourage most of its sales to come from the area. It is easier to justify in the sense that there can be some overlapping competition with neighboring distributors.

There are also clauses in some distributor agreements that provide for compensation to a distributor who has a particular area of responsibility and has lost sales to another distributor of the same product. If, for example, customer A lives in Ohio, which is the area of primary responsibility of distributor 1 of product X, and is solicited for sale by and purchases product X from distributor 2 from Indiana, then distributor 2 is required to pay distributor 1 a certain fee for having made the sale. The rationale behind the clause is that distributor 1, through its concentrated promotional and advertising efforts, has promoted product X and distributor 2 has benefited by selling to customer A. The intent is to encourage promotion of the supplier's products by its distributors. Such a clause in and of itself may not be illegal and would be looked at as part of the other restrictions upon the distributor and reviewed under the rule-of-reason test. Again, this clause would be only one factor considered by the courts in balancing between the procompetitive and anticompetitive aspects.

Other restrictions such as hours the distributor or franchisee will be open, advertising requirements, quality of ingredients, sales goals, minimum inventory supply, and architecture of a new building are usually permissible as long as they are reasonable in nature. They usually have limited impact upon competition.

Generally, any non-price restriction placed on a distributor or franchisee by the supplier or franchiser relating to its operation as a business would be looked at to see if it unreasonably restrained trade (rule-of-reason test). Exceptions would be certain tying arrangements, reciprocity agreements and, of course, any pricing restrictions.

### Tying arrangement

Basically, a *tying arrangement* involves a situation in which a seller conditions the sale of one item (the tying item) upon the purchase by the potential buyer of a second item (the tied item). Today, there are many situations which could involve tying arrangements. Supplier-distributor, franchiser-franchisee, and the basic seller-buyer relationships can invite attempts to tie the sale of a weak, slow-moving or readily available product with a unique, competitively superior, or highly demanded product. For example, in a fast-food franchise arrangement, the franchiser may desire that the franchisee agree to purchase all of its supplies from the franchiser in order to obtain the franchise and the use of the trade name or trademark.

The courts have stated that tying arrangements serve no valid competitive purpose and are therefore per se illegal under the antitrust laws. For example, the U.S. Supreme Court stated:

> Where such conditions (tying arrangements) are successfully exacted competition on the merits with respect to the tied product is inevitably curbed. Indeed "tying agreements serve hardly any purpose beyond the suppression of competition." . . . They deny competitors free access to the market for the tied product not because the party imposing the tying requirements has a better product or a lower price, but because of his power or leverage in another market. At the same time buyers are forced to forego their free choice between competing products.[7]

The tied items need not be sold by the seller; they can be items sold by a certain limited number of other sellers designated by the seller of the tying item. For example, the seller may require that all accessories, supplies, or services be purchased only from a designated company. If those items are readily available elsewhere, then the arrangement will be considered a tying one if the requirements discussed below are met.

A tying arrangement may fall under coverage of section 1 of the Sherman Act, section 3 of the Clayton Act, and/or section 5 of the FTC Act. It is outside the scope of this book to discuss and analyze when certain conduct would fall within each particular section. However, it is important for you to understand the basic concept of a tying arrangement and that the arrangement is generally considered per se illegal under the antitrust laws no matter under which of the three sections it may fall.

The basic requirements to a finding of a tying arrangement are:[8]

1. That there be at least two separate items that are tied together.
2. That the seller has sufficient economic power in the tying item that it can thereby appreciably restrain competition in the market for the tied item (force the tie).
3. That a not insubstantial amount of interstate commerce in the tied item is affected.

The question of two separate items can arise in situations in which a "package" is being sold; an example is a franchise package involving the use of the trademark and the sale of certain needed equipment and supplies. Trademark licenses, patent licenses, credit, services, and other items that can be and are sold separately may be considered separate items. However, whether the package is really one item or two or more items depends upon the facts of the particular situation. The courts will consider such factors as whether the items are sold separately in separate markets and whether they have different or distinct characteristics or physical properties. An example of the latter is maintenance service on technologically complex equipment.

The question of separateness arises frequently in franchise arrangements. Since the trademark license can be a separate item, the question is whether, under a particular franchise arrangement, the trademark should be considered part of one package item or a separate item and the other purchase requirements placed on the franchisee be considered tied items.

Another example of the imposition of a tie is when two products are substantially cheaper if purchased together than if purchased separately and there is no real cost justification for the lower price. If this has the effect of causing the tied product to be continuously purchased with the tying product, then a court may find that a tie was imposed.

The next basic question is whether the tying arrangement was imposed upon the buyer by the seller through some form of economic power of the seller or was voluntarily entered into by the buyer. The courts generally have concluded that the possession of patents and trademarks is to be considered the possession of economic power and therefore gives the seller the power to force a tie with the trademark or patent. In addition, the courts will look at the uniqueness of the tying product, the demand for it, any competitive products, any substitutable products, and any other relevant factors to determine if the seller has the economic power to require the sale of the tied product along with the tying product.

Therefore, you need to be careful of:

- Requiring that any two distinct products be sold only together or at prices greatly reduced from separate sales and without cost justification.
- Licensing any patent rights, trademarks, trade names, or copyrights in conjunction with any other products, including other patent rights, trademarks, trade names, or copyright licenses.
- Refusing to sell products separately but requiring that the buyer agree to purchase your entire line.
- Requiring that a service contract on the product be purchased at the same time as the product is sold.
- Designating specific sellers from whom the buyer must obtain certain other widely available products.
- Requiring that certain widely available products be purchased from your company as part of the sale of a unique or highly desirable product by your company.

There is a recognized limited defense that makes certain otherwise illegal tie-ins permissible. That is when no substitute products equal in quality to the tied product are available and the tied product is needed to ensure the proper operation of the tying product.[9] For example, a company could require that engineering services needed for the maintenance of certain equipment be purchased from the seller at the time of the sale of the equipment because the equipment is considered complex or is in its early stages of technological advance and no other firm qualified to provide competent service exists.[10]

A company could also prove that its future existence depended upon building up goodwill that might be shattered without the tie-in arrangement. This exception is a recognition that when one product (say, a trademark) requires use of a second product (say, food), the quality of that second product is vital to the preservation of the goodwill of the company, and no other substitutable products of equal quality are available, then such a tie-in arrangement would probably be acceptable to the courts. For example, it may be acceptable for a fast-food franchise operation to require that a certain quality of food be purchased from the franchiser, since it may be impossible to control the quality of the particular food that might otherwise be bought by the franchisee. But it would be difficult to justify any tie-in requirement on paper supplies, the quality of which can vary somewhat and not be damaging to the goodwill. However, if the quality of the food involved need not be strictly controlled or maintained, then such a defense would not apply.

### Reciprocal sales or purchases between a supplier and a purchaser

In a reciprocal dealing arrangement, one company buys from a second on the condition that that second company buy from the first. Such an agreement or understanding would most likely be illegal under the antitrust laws. Any reciprocal dealing between two companies that "I will buy from you if you buy from me" is illegal. It forecloses competition for the sales involved and is therefore anticompetitive and has generally been found by the courts to be a per se violation. For example, company A buys xods as a needed supply and can buy them from several suppliers, but it develops an understanding that it will buy its xods from company L because company L will buy the yings it needs from company A in exchange for company A's purchasing the xods from company L. Obviously, reciprocal dealings would only occur when at least one of the companies was diversified enough to need and/or produce more than one product, since single-product firms are not likely to need each other's products.

Under the antitrust laws it is illegal for two companies to have some type of understanding to deal on a reciprocal basis with each other. The understanding may be reached through coercion by use of the purchasing power of one of the companies or by a mutual uncoerced agreement between the two companies. Obviously, there must be evidence of the understanding or agreement before there is a violation. Part of the evidence, besides the actual buying of each other's products, could be documents keeping track of purchases and sales, use of a "trade relations" department, or having the same employee purchase from and sell to the other company.

It is not illegal to decide independently to buy from a particular company in the hope that it may purchase from you, provided there is no understanding that the purchases will continue or that the amounts will be determined by the purchases made by one company from the other.

As in the other areas of antitrust, an agreement or understanding can be implied by the court or jury from circumstantial evidence. A reciprocity agreement could therefore be implied from conduct, documents, or economic theories. As a result, you should consider the following:

• Do not make any threats to withdraw purchases in order to force reciprocal sales onto your supplier.

• Be careful of having in your company a "trade relations" department which might involve comparing purchases and sales with a particular supplier–customer.

• Be careful of centralizing the purchasing and selling functions for your company in the same individuals.

• If the purchasing and selling functions are assigned to the same group of individuals, make sure that the same individual does not both sell to and buy from the same supplier–customer.

• Be careful of any threats, implications, innuendos, or other attempts at coercing your supplier into purchasing from you for the reason that you are purchasing from it.

• Any evidence of continued purchases from a customer

despite higher prices, poorer product quality, or poorer service may be an indication of some form of reciprocity agreement.

Although there may be some question in the court opinions as to whether an absolute per se rule is to be applied, it is important for you to know that reciprocity agreements have been determined to be per se illegal under the antitrust laws in many circumstances when a "not insubstantial" amount of commerce has been involved. What is a not insubstantial amount of commerce is a fact question for the court or jury. Basically, if more than a minimal amount of commerce is involved, the reciprocal arrangement runs the risk of being considered per se illegal.

### Exclusive-dealing contract; requirements contract

The term often used to describe a situation in which a seller conditions the sale of its product on the buyer's agreement not to buy the product from any competitor of the seller is an *exclusive-dealing contract.* The term often used to describe a situation in which the buyer agrees to purchase all of a particular product only from a particular seller for a specified period of time or in which a seller agrees to supply all of the buyer's demands for a particular product for a specified period of time is a *requirements contract.*

There is no essential difference between an exclusive-dealing contract and a requirements contract for purposes of compliance with or violation of the antitrust laws, and therefore, generally speaking, it is not important to determine how an arrangement should be labeled. Both an exclusive-dealing and a requirements contract rest upon the same underlying fact: the supplier and purchaser have agreed that the supplier will sell and the purchaser will buy all of the purchaser's needs of a particular product or of the supplier's production.

A buyer and/or seller may wish to enter into an exclusive-dealing arrangement for many reasons; it may, for example, wish to have a guaranteed outlet or supply a hedge against future shortage, or an exclusive distributor or sole franchisee in a particular geographic area. The concern of the antitrust laws is that such an arrangement may have an anticompetitive effect in that it excludes the seller's competitors from sales to the captive buyer for the period of the agreement and that the buyer is not free to choose to buy the product from the seller's competitors.

Exclusive-dealing arrangements are subject to antitrust review under section 1 of the Sherman Act, section 3 of the Clayton Act, and section 5 of the FTC Act. Since the arrangement obviously forecloses a portion of the market to the supplier's competitors, it may be violative of any of those sections. The test of illegality under the Clayton Act is whether the arrangement substantially lessens competition in the relevant market. The test under section 1 of the Sherman Act and basically also under the FTC Act is the rule of reason.

Thus the basic test to determine if there is an antitrust violation is the rule-of-reason. Although the tests under the three sections may have different labels, they are basically the same. Any distinctions are not relevant to the purpose of this book: to give you a general understanding of the antitrust laws.

The rule-of-reason test determines whether there will be a substantial adverse effect upon competition in the particular market. To determine that, the court needs to know what the market is. It looks at both the geographic market and the product market. The geographic market is the area in which the seller can compete effectively in selling the particular product. The product market includes all products that would compete with the particular product subject to the exclusive-dealing arrangement.

The determination of a product market would take into consideration the substitutability, similarity of use, and acceptability of interchangeability by purchasers. The market, in and of itself, is usually difficult to ascertain. Once it is determined, however, the court needs to determine if the restraint is an unreasonable restriction within that market.

Unreasonability is ascertained by one of two possible tests. The *quantitative test* looks primarily at the percent of the market foreclosed, that is, the percent that is held by the "locked-in" product subject to the exclusive-dealing arrangement. Depending upon other facts, as little as 7 percent of the market could be held sufficient to find a restraint unreasonable.[11] That does not mean that 7 percent will be so held; it means only that as little as 7 percent has been held sufficient.

A second test often used, and used more often today, is the *qualitative test*,[12] which determines the effect upon the market by looking at such factors as percent of market share controlled by the exclusive-dealing contract, the existence of present competitors and ease of entry into the market by new competitors, business reasons for the contract, strength of the parties involved, length of the contract, and whether any permanent changes within the industry structure will result.

Basically, then, the court will look at the procompetitive and anticompetitive aspects of any such arrangement and determine if, over all, the arrangement is anticompetitive. That does not give you any concrete guidance when looking at potential or present exclusive-dealing arrangements, but it is what the courts use to determine whether an arrangement violates the antitrust laws. If your company on its own chooses to buy all of its needs for a particular product from one supplier, the question of a possible unreasonable anticompetitive restraint is not raised unless the decision is part of an attempt to monopolize a particular market by your company.

Exclusive dealing may arise in a situation in which you agree to supply all of a customer s needs for a particular part manufactured by your company or to supply to a customer your entire output of a particular ingredient which you process. The situations could be reversed. The supplier of a particular part may agree to supply all your needs for that part, or you may agree to purchase a supplier's entire output of a particular ingredient.

Antitrust questions can be and are raised by exclusive distributor arrangements under which the distributor is the exclusive purchaser and reseller of the supplier's product. The supplier agrees to sell all of a particular product to a particular buyer (the exclusive distributor) in a particular geographic area. Sometimes such an arrangement will include an agreement by the distributor not to carry any competing lines. (See also discussions in other parts of this chapter that deal with other questions involving distributors, including exclusive distributorships.)

To require that a buyer not handle competing lines may unreasonably restrain competition by substantially lessening it. However, if there are other adequate outlets for the products of the seller's competitors and the buyer's share of the market for that product is small, then the restraint may not be unreasonable. Evidence of procompetitive effects also are helpful. For example, there may be evidence that a prohibition against handling competing lines actually encourages competition between the seller's product and the products of its competitors sold through other outlets because the distributor can concentrate his efforts on promoting, selling, and servicing that particular brand and thereby increase interbrand competition.

Another common situation in which an exclusive dealing question may arise is that in which a buyer wants exclusive rights to sell a particular product or product line. A third common situation is the typical franchise arrangement whereby a franchisee is given exclusive rights to sell its franchised product within a particular area.

Most exclusive arrangements will be valid if competing brands or products are available to others, the supplier does not have a monopoly in the product or product line, the other buyers have alternative sources of supply, and no unreasonable restraint of trade is shown by the particular facts.

There is no requirement that the buyer or supplier must be coerced into the arrangement or must voluntarily have entered into it. Under either situation the arrangement would be subject to review. However, the economic or business reason why the party entered into the arrangement is one factor the court could consider under the above-discussed test.

The above discussion should point out to you the complexity in determining the legality or illegality of a particular exclusive-dealing arrangement. Therefore, consultation with your attorney on any such arrangement is prudent.

### Franchising and business opportunity ventures—FTC trade regulation rule

The FTC has issued an extensive trade regulation rule entitled *Franchising and Business Opportunity Ventures.*[13] The rule covers disclosure requirements to prospective franchisees. The FTC had considered some form of the rule for 7 years prior to its actual adoption.

The rule requires the disclosure, in a prospectus, of 20 different areas of information, including the following:

1. Identifying information as to franchiser.
2. Business experience of franchiser's directors and executive officers.
3. Business experience of the franchiser.
4. Litigation history.
5. Bankruptcy history.
6. Description of franchise.
7. Initial funds required to be paid by a franchisee.
8. Recurring funds required to be paid by a franchisee.
9. Affiliated persons the franchisee is required or advised to do business with by the franchiser.
10. Obligations to purchase.
11. Revenues received by the franchiser in consideration of purchases by a franchisee.
12. Financing arrangements.
13. Restriction of sales.
14. Personal participation required of the franchisee in the operation of the franchise.
15. Termination, cancellation, and renewal of the franchise.
16. Statistical information concerning the number of franchises and company-owned outlets.
17. Site selection.
18. Training programs.
19. Public figures involvement in the franchise.
20. Financial information concerning the franchiser.

The rule is directed at disclosure in the advertising, offering, licensing, contracting, sale, or other promotion in or affecting commerce of any franchise or any relationship which is represented to be a franchise. The rule defines "franchise," "franchiser," and other key words. It could have broad application.

In addition to the extensive disclosure regulation, the rule also provides a private cause of action to anyone injured by a violation of the rule. The extent of that right is presently unknown. However, if your company is a franchiser, it would be wise to determine whether the rule is applicable to it and, if so, to comply with its various requirements. Otherwise, your company runs the risk of not only an FTC enforcement action but also a private cause of action.

## REFERENCES

1. *Dr. Miles Medical Co. v. John D. Park & Sons,* 220 U.S. 373(1911).
2. 250 U.S. 300(1919).
3. *United States v. Parke, Davis & Co.,* 362 U.S. 29(1960).
4. *Simpson v. Union Oil Co.,* 377 U.S. 13(1964).
5. *Klor's v. Broadway-Hale Stores,* 359 U.S. 207(1959).
6. 433 U.S. 36(1977).
7. *Northern Pacific Ry. v. United States,* 356 U.S. 1, 6(1958).
8. *Fortner Enterprises v. United States,* 429 U.S. 610(1977).
9. *Dehydrating Process Co. v. A. O. Smith Corp.,* 292 F. 2d 653 (1st Cir.), cert. denied 368 U.S. 931(1961).
10. *United States v. Jerrold Electronics Corp.,* 187 F. Supp. 545 (E.D. Pa. 1960); aff'd. per curiam, 365 U.S. 567(1961).
11. *Standard Oil Co. & Standard Stations v. United States,* 337 U.S. 293(1949).
12. *Tampa Electric Co. v. Nashville Coal Co.,* 365 U.S. 320(1961).
13. 16 C.F.R. sec. 476 et. seq. (eff. 10/21/79).

# 6

# Discrimination in prices, promotional and advertising allowances, and services

The Robinson-Patman Act[1] was passed to prevent discrimination in prices, improper use of brokerage fees, and discrimination in promotional and advertising allowances and services. Its primary aim was to prevent large buyers such as supermarket chains from using their purchasing leverage to obtain prices lower than were available to other competing purchasers. Certain exceptions were placed into the Act to permit differences in prices when certain conditions are met. Also, certain discriminatory acts are considered a crime. The Act places liability upon both a knowing buyer and a knowing seller who violate it.

## Discrimination in price

Basically, you can not sell the same product to two purchasers at different prices unless there is a justification (as discussed later in this chapter) for the price difference.

Section 2(a) of the Robinson-Patman Act prohibits any seller engaged in commerce to directly or indirectly discriminate in the price it charges different purchasers on the sale of commodities of like grade and quality when such discrimination may substantially lessen competition or tend to create a monopoly in any line of commerce or cause competitive injury to the purchasers' competitors or its customers' competitors. That raises several factual and legal questions that must be determined when any particular situation is reviewed. They include what is meant by these terms: discriminate, price, purchasers, sale, commodities, like grade and quality, in any line of commerce, and competitive injury.

The price compared is the actual net price to the customer—what the customer actually pays after discounts, allowances, or rebates. Discrimination may occur when any different services, credit terms, delivery, return privileges, freight terms, or free goods are provided to different competing purchasers.

It is not necessary that each buyer take advantage of any particular discount, allowance, or rebate. What is important is that you make discounts and so on available to all potential buyers to the extent discussed below—that is, do not discriminate.

Sometimes the question is whether use of certain delivered pricing, freight allowances, pick-up allowances or similar transportation allowances creates discrimination in prices. That can often lead to complex factual questions in determining whether certain customers are receiving lower net prices, because customer location creates a difference in transportation costs. Basically, you should make any allowance choice available to all, and any freight costs should be plugged into any delivered-price system. However, there are situations in which certain of the "fringes" need not be offered to all. One occurs when the customer is performing a service, such as a wholesale function, and earns a discount for that service.

A parent-subsidiary relationship can raise several questions. One question that may arise is whether a sale by a parent company and a sale by one of its subsidiaries to competing customers would be considered two sales by the same "person" under the Act. Generally, the parent-subsidiary would be considered the same person only if the parent exercised complete control over the subsidiary and left the subsidiary with little or no separate management authority, including pricing authority.

A second question that may arise is whether a transaction between a parent and its subsidiary would be considered a sale for these purposes. There is some dispute among the courts, but generally the transaction would most likely be considered a sale if it were made at arm's length or the subsidiary (purchaser) were a competitor of other purchasers from the parent.

### Geographic pricing requirements

If your company competes in several marketing territories, then, unless a variance is justified, you must sell in all territories at the same price. A variance would be justified if your company were meeting the price competition of a company located and competing only in a particular geographic area. Since, generally, there would not be an adverse effect upon competition in that geographic area, such a price difference would not be considered violative of the Robinson-Patman Act. That is especially true when you are competing in a homogeneous product market.

However, if your product has qualities that dictate a higher price and you selectively reduce the price in certain markets, then there may be problems. In fact, generally, such action may raise a question of violation if it is shown that you selected certain markets in which to sell at low prices to drive a competitor out of business. If you sell below cost, subsidize low prices in one market by higher prices in another, or express an attempt to do so, then it may be presumed by the court that your intent is to drive out a competitor by illegal means, that is, by predatory practices. It will be a violation of the Robinson-Patman Act as well as possible evidence of an attempt to monopolize or an illegal attempt to drive a particular competitor out of the market.

### Injury to competitors or to a customer's competitors

Primary-line injury is injury to competitors of the company that sold at discriminatory prices. Secondary-line injury is injury to the competitors of the customer that received the discriminatory prices. Thus, to look at the adverse effect on competition, one looks not only at the effect on the competitors of the company in question but also at the effect on the competitors of the company's customer. If there is injury to any member of either group, there may be a violation.

A secondary-line injury must be to a customer's competitors within the same market. In other words, if there are two customers who receive different prices but are in separate markets, then there is no secondary-line injury. Customers or competitors of your customer must show not only a discrimination in price but also that they suffered financial injury as a result of the discrimination.

Injury to a seller's competitors (primary-line injury) is often determined by looking at the prices to see if they would be considered predatory. Exactly what predatory pricing is has not yet been totally answered. Some courts say that pricing below marginal cost is predatory; others say that pricing below average variable cost is predatory. However predatory pricing is ultimately defined and however any cost formula is ultimately defined, you should remember that if your company is pricing so far below its normal range for a product that it is foregoing short-term profits, the action should be reviewed immediately to determine whether the prices are legal. Therefore, consult your attorney before making any major price move, especially a move that is localized.

You are permitted to be competitive—after all, the purpose of the antitrust laws is to encourage competition—but there can be a fine line between being competitive and being predatory and causing primary-line competitive injury.

Sometimes under particular factual circumstances the court may assume competitive injury, especially at the secondary level in a highly competitive situation. Other times the court will look at the competitive situation to determine if there has been injury. Therefore, no general rule on the extent of proof necessary to show competitive injury can be set forth.

### Definitions

"Two different purchases" means purchases within the same geographic market. It also means two sales are needed. A lease, license, royalty, or offer to sell is not a "sale." Even that gets fuzzy if the transaction looks, overall, more like a sale. For example, a long-term lease with an option to buy may be considered a sale by the court.

"Commodities" basically means tangible goods (products) as contrasted to services or intangibles such as bank loans, patented processes, construction contracts, "tolling" agreements, and radio or TV advertising.

"Like grade and quality" basically means products that are physically and chemically identical even though they have different labels and different acceptance by consumers. The test is *commercial identity* or *commercial fungibility;* it thus depends upon the particular products being sold. If special-order items are being sold with customized parts or sizes and no two are physically alike, that is, there are bona fide physical differences which affect marketability, then there is no commercial identity or commercial fungibility and therefore the same product is not being sold to two purchasers.

### Defenses to a charge of price discrimination[2]

*Cost Justification.* The statute permits a price difference that is due to a difference in costs of manufacture, sale, or delivery of the product resulting from the methods by or quantities in which the goods are sold or delivered. Cost justification need not be analyzed on a customer-by-customer basis. The costs for a group of customers with similar characteristics can be averaged and used to justify any discrimination between a customer who is a member of that group and another customer who is not.[3]

The cost justification defense applies to a price discrimination but not to a charge of unlawful brokerage payment, discrimination in advertising, or promotional services or facilities, which are discussed later in this chapter.

*Meeting Competition.* A defendant can show that its lower price (discriminatory price) was made "in good faith to meet an equally low price of a competitor." That is an absolute defense. It means that, if it is shown to be true, there is no violation of the statute by the seller. However, the seller must act in good faith in meeting its competitor's price. Also, the seller can only meet and not beat the competitor's price.

You should not check with the competitor or other competitors to determine if you are meeting a real price. As long as you act in good faith and reasonably use other means to authenticate the competitor's price, you should have a valid defense. You could, for example, obtain a copy of any bid, proposal, or invoice given to the customer by the competitor.

To keep a record of meeting competitors' prices, your company should have standard forms to be filled out to explain why the sales person feels a lower price is needed to meet competition. In addition to the explanation, a copy of any documentation (such as a copy of the competitor's bid or proposal) from the customer or elsewhere should be attached. The record can be extremely helpful in successfully defending a price discrimination case based upon a meeting-competition defense. Direct verification of prices for a meeting-competition defense is not an excuse to communicate with a competitor. Such a communication can easily be construed as evidence of price-fixing activities.

*Changing Conditions.* Price change made "in response to changing conditions affecting the market for or marketability of goods concerned, such as but not limited to actual or imminent deterioration of perishable goods, obsolescence of seasonal goods, distress sales under court process, or sales in good faith in discontinuance of business in goods concerned"[4] is another defense. It is basically self-explanatory; it permits a seller to change its prices in response to a change in the market for or the marketability of the goods. The change must be made in good faith, and the burden is on the seller to prove the facts to fit the defense as available.

## Buyer's liability

The above discussion covered the seller's liability for discriminatory pricing. Section 2(f) states that "it shall be unlawful for any person engaged in commerce, in the course of such commerce, knowingly to induce or receive a discrimination in price which is prohibited by this section."[5] Basically, the provision prohibits a buyer from forcing a seller to sell, or deceiving a seller into selling, a product to the buyer at a discriminatorily low price.

In a "lying buyer" situation (in which the buyer lies about a competitor's price), the FTC is required to show that the buyer knew or should have known that the price was discriminatory and that the seller would not have a valid defense. However, it is permitted to show this through trade experience. The FTC has brought actions against both the seller and the buyer, alleging that both violated the Robinson-Patman Act.

There is some legal question today about whether a buyer can be found liable for inducing a sale when a seller has a valid defense based on cost justification or meeting competition (or at least when the seller is led by the buyer to believe it is meeting competition).[6] However, the caution still is there. Do not attempt to induce a discriminatory price or accept one when you have knowledge that the price is unjustifiably lower than others are receiving. At the very least, your company's defense would be based upon the strength of any defense the seller would have. That would be an awkward position to put your company in, and it might invite both government and private treble damage lawsuits.

### Improper use of broker's fees

Section 2(c) prohibits

> any person . . . to pay or grant, or to receive or accept, anything of value as a commission, brokerage, or other compensation, or any allowance or discount in lieu thereof except for services rendered in connection with the sale or purchase of goods, wares, [or] merchandise.

The purpose of this provision was to prohibit rebates disguised as broker's fees.

Basically, a seller cannot pay a phony broker's fee to a buyer or an agent of the buyer. There cannot be a split of the broker's fees, or a reduction in payment of the fee, as a means of reducing the price to the buyer. Either would amount to a discriminatory price to the buyer; the price to the buyer would be less than paid by competitors without any cost savings to justify the reduction.

If the buyer performs a function such as warehousing, then it can receive a functional discount. What is to be avoided is a price reduction that cannot be justified by cost savings or a functional discount.

The other defenses that are available to a charge of price discrimination, such as meeting competition, are not available here.

## Promotional allowances and services

Sections 2(d) and 2(e) prohibit a seller from giving promotional allowances or services to or for the benefit of a customer unless the allowance or service is available on proportionally equal terms to all other customers competing in the distribution of the products. Basically, the action prohibited has been determined to be a per se violation with no defense other than that of meeting competition.

The FTC has issued *Guides for Advertising Allowances and Other Merchandising Payments and Services*[7] to assist businesses in complying with this area of the law. The law applies to situations which involve a sale to a customer who buys for resale. The requirement that allowances be available on proportionally equal terms applies to customers that compete in the resale of the seller's goods. Which customers compete is determined on a geographic and functional basis. That applies whether your customers buy direct or from a wholesaler or both.[8]

You can use a wholesaler to implement a promotional allowance program, but your company is responsible for all competing customers being generally aware. To keep equality between direct and indirect buyers, you are required to advise your indirect customers of any such promotional allowances. You can notify your customers by whatever means you like, but it would be wise to do so in a manner that provides your company with documentation of the method of notifying all customers. It is not required that all customers use such allowances; it is only necessary that the allowances be available on proportionally equal terms.

What constitutes "proportionally equal terms" is difficult to ascertain, as even the FTC *Guides* acknowledge. The general rule is that the allowances be made available to competing customers on the basis of the cost of the service in relation to the dollar volume or quantity of goods purchased by the particular customer. However, other methods which are fair to all competing customers are also acceptable.

Even if a particular situation does not fall within the coverage of section 2(c), as when the allowances are not connected to the resale of the product, it may still be price discrimination under the Act. In other words, disguising an allowance that pertains to your sale to the customer and calling it a freight allowance or a term of credit may keep it out from under section 2(c), but it would then fall under the section prohibiting price discrimination.

The meeting-competition defense is generally permitted to substantiate the provision of a promotional service to one customer and not another or to one customer to a greater extent than to another. If your company has a lawful promotional plan and you deviate from it for a customer in order to meet competition, the deviation will most likely be permitted. Remember to document any meeting-competition action and the development of any promotional plan.

### Criminal sanctions[9]

For certain discriminatory conduct the Robinson-Patman Act provides criminal sanctions. Three basic types of conduct are prohibited:

1. Overall price discrimination:

It shall be unlawful for any person . . . to be a party to, or assist in, any transaction of sale, or contract to sell, which discriminates to his knowledge against competitors of the purchaser, in that, any discount, rebate, allowance, or advertising service charge is granted to the purchaser over and above any discount, rebate, allowance, or advertising service charge available at the time of such transaction to said competitors in respect of a sale of goods of like grade, quality, and quantity.

2. Territorial price discrimination with the purpose of eliminating competition:

It shall be unlawful for any person . . . to sell, or contract to sell, goods in any part of the United States at prices lower than those exacted by said person elsewhere in the United States for the purpose of destroying competition, or eliminating a competitor in such part of the United States.

3. Sales at unreasonably low prices (predatory prices) for purpose of eliminating competition:

It shall be unlawful for any person . . . to sell, or contract to sell, goods at unreasonably low prices for the purpose of destroying competition or eliminating a competitor.

Any person convicted can be fined up to $5,000 or imprisoned up to one year, or both. The Antitrust Division has sole enforcement authority. The U.S. Supreme Court has found that this section does not provide a cause of action for private parties and is not within the enforcement authority of the FTC. It was passed as a separate act and was not part of the amendment to the Clayton Act.

The use of section 3 as an enforcement tool has been somewhat limited so far and primarily against sellers; but it can cover buyers. The person must "know" the discrimination exists, and the discrimination must involve goods of like grade, quality, and quantity. The restriction against territorial price discrimination applies to prices that are lower in one part of the United States than another for the purpose of eliminating competition or a competitor. If the lower prices are intended to meet competition because of lower costs or some other legitimate business reason, then they are not for the prohibited purpose.

What is meant by "unreasonably low prices" is unclear. Selling below cost (however that is defined) most likely would be considered "unreasonably low prices," especially if such prices continued for a long period of time. The purpose of eliminating competition or a competitor is usually proved by conduct; thus the low prices themselves would be evidence of that purpose. The entry of a new, vulnerable competitor immediately prior to the lowering of the prices would be additional evidence. Internal memoranda stating that the company will "regain the market" or "drive the competitors out" would certainly be evidence.

It is important for you to remember that the provision is there. The Antitrust Division can and has used it. Government antitrust enforcement agencies are continuously looking for more effective ways to eliminate anticompetitive conduct. If sometime in the future the Antitrust Division concludes that this provision can be a useful tool, it will begin using it more often. Your company certainly does not want to be one of the defendants.

### Enforcement of the Robinson-Patman Act

The Antitrust Division has decreased its enforcement efforts of the Robinson-Patman Act. The Division's position basically is that the Act's provisions do not always foster competition and therefore enforcement of the Act runs counter to the goals of the other antitrust statutes. The FTC still enforces the Act, other than the criminal section for which it has no authority.

Private parties who may have been injured as a result of activity that violates the Act have a right of action for treble damages. That is the most frequent use of the provisions of the Act. Thus a violation of the Act could invite a lawsuit from your competitors or the competitors of your favored buyer.

## REFERENCES

1.  15 U.S.C. sec. 13 (sec. 2 of the Clayton Act).
2.  15 U.S.C. sec. 13(b) [sec. 2(b) of the Clayton Act].
3.  *United States v. Bowman Dairy Co.* and *United States v. Borden Co.*, both at 370 U.S. 460(1969).
4.  15 U.S.C. sec. 13(a) [sec. 2(a) of the Clayton Act].
5.  15 U.S.C. sec. 13(f) [sec. 2(f) of the Clayton Act].
6.  *Great Atlantic & Pacific Tea Co. v. FTC,* 59 L. Ed. 2d 153.
7.  16 C.F.R. sec. 240(1973).
8.  *F.T.C. v. Fred Meyer, Inc.,* 390 U.S. 341(1968).
9.  15 U.S.C. sec. 13a (sec. 3 of the Robinson-Patman Act).

# 7

# Conduct resulting in monopoly questions

## What companies would be covered

You may think that "monopoly" applies only to the IBM's of the world. It is a part of the antitrust law that is of concern to companies with a large percentage of a particular market (however "market" is defined) and to any company that, in general, is considered a "large" company. But it also can be applicable to companies much smaller than those types of businesses. It can be applicable because "small" companies themselves can be charged with monopolizing or attempting to monopolize and because smaller companies have certain rights under the antitrust laws as protection against being driven out of business by an alleged monopolist.

Section 2 of the Sherman Act makes it a violation for a company to "monopolize, or attempt to monopolize, or combine or conspire to monopolize" any part of interstate or foreign commerce. The mere fact that a company has a "monopoly" position in a particular "market" does not mean that, in and of itself, is a violation of section 2 of the Sherman Act. What is important is how a company obtains and/or maintains its monopoly position.

Before we look at the basic explanation of the relevant

elements of a monopoly violation, let us see how a violation might apply to companies different in size. First, you don't necessarily have to be large, that is, have a large net worth, net income, or asset value or meet any other financial yardstick to be subject to a monopoly charge. Any company of any size that is dominant in a particular market could become involved. As we will see, "market" generally includes a geographic limitation. For example, it might be that under certain fact situations the geographic market area is limited to a city or its metropolitan area. An example might be the market for taxi service, dry cleaning, or home delivery of diapers or newspapers, assuming the interstate requirements are met. Likewise, your company may be dominant even nationally in a particular product line, such as specialty items used in the automotive industry.

Thus a company that is very small as measured by the various financial yardsticks can still be subject to the concerns of monopolization. Furthermore, many state statutes include a monopolization section, so that firms within a state, even though small on a national scale, would be subject to antitrust review by that state on monopoly questions. That is especially true when the geographic market is statewide or smaller.

As a practical matter, if a company in a particular state is suspected of attempting to monopolize in a market larger than the state, the case will generally be referred to the Antitrust Division of the Department of Justice or the Federal Trade Commission even if it is first looked into by the state. That is true for three principal reasons: the resources, expertise, and broader geographic reach of investigative discovery authority of the federal agencies.

On the other side of the coin are the rights of companies, especially smaller companies, to expect dominant companies within a particular market to act in compliance with the antitrust laws, including the portions covering monopolization. If a company is in violation of section 2 and your company has been damaged thereby, it has a right to three times the damages plus injunctive or other relief to remove the effect of the monopoly conduct.

It is important to point out here that generally a suit

alleging monopolization or an attempt to monopolize is very time-consuming and expensive. It can last for years and cost hundreds of thousands of dollars. Naturally, that depends upon the lawsuit. There are suits in which relatively small companies have brought actions against larger companies charging attempts to monopolize or monopolization. To say that you have certain rights is correct, but it is also correct to say that to enforce those rights may be not only very time-consuming and expensive but also frustrating.

### Monopolization

Let us look at the elements making up a charge of monopolization. We will not analyze any of the elements in depth; instead, we will look at the legal issues in a charge of monopolization so that you can have a basic understanding of why certain conduct by your company may create monopoly problems. The basic elements are:

1. Possession of monopoly power in the relevant market.
2. The willful acquisition or maintenance of that power as distinguished from growth or development as a consequence of a superior product, business acumen, or historic accident.[1]

*Monopoly power* is the power to control prices or exclude competition. *Relevant market* includes all products that are reasonably interchangeable for the purposes for which they were produced, taking into consideration price, use, and quality (the *product market*).[2] It also includes the geographic area of competition for that product (the *geographic market*). That may include an area broader than the defendant's present selling area.

Although easily defined in the abstract, the product and geographic markets are often very difficult to ascertain in an actual situation. For example, if the defendant manufactures casual 100 percent cotton slacks, is that the product market? Or do you include dress slacks, jeans, suit pants, tennis shorts, polyester slacks, and 50 percent cotton slacks? Likewise, if the defendant sells only in a six-state area, should there be a larger geographic area because casual slacks are sold nationally?

The defendant is always interested in expanding the definitions of the product and geographic markets because that will reduce its percent of the relevant market. The plaintiff is interested in narrowing the market definition because that will increase the defendant's share of the market.

How such power was obtained or maintained is then reviewed. If it was obtained or retained through reasonable business practices, that is, from "superior skill, foresight and industry," it would not be illegally acquired or maintained. The court will look at the conduct of the company to determine intent and purpose. If the conduct is predatory—practices such as below cost pricing, restrictive contracts, and unreasonable control of raw supplies—the court may find that it, when coupled with monopoly power, shows the intent and purpose to monopolize.

There is constant debate, which is even more heated today than previously, that monopoly power per se should be prohibited, irrespective of how it is obtained. The argument goes that such power can give rise to pricing manipulation by the monopolist and control over entry of competitors and that it is not in the best interest of our social and economic system to permit so much power in any particular market. There is even concern over the total size of a company without regard to whether the company has monopoly power within a particular market. So far, size of a company itself does not make the acts of the company illegal, although large or dominant companies may create a suspicion of monopoly power by their mere size. Therefore, caution is in order when one becomes dominant in a particular product or market.

Determining the percent of the market held by the defendant is nothing more than a means for the court to determine whether there is monopoly power under section 2 of the Sherman Act. What is monopoly power as measured by percent of market depends upon the facts, the industry, and the products involved. However, there is case language that says 90 percent definitely is and 33 percent certainly is not.[3] Whether those would be the outer limits in every situation is not known; that still depends upon the facts of each case.

### Attempt to monopolize

Basically, a charge of attempt to monopolize alleges that, although the defendant has not obtained a monopoly in a particular market (the relevant market), it had a specific intent to achieve a monopoly and that, based upon certain conduct of the defendant, there is a dangerous probability that it would establish one in the relevant market.

The definitions and proofs of the relevant product and geographic markets are basically the same as under monopolization. In some cases a question is raised as to whether there is a need to show a relevant market as part of any proof of an attempt to monopolize. The specific intent can be inferred from the defendant's conduct.

The courts are often quick to point out that a fine line has to be drawn between conduct aimed at attempting to monopolize and the healthy, aggressive, competitive conduct that the antitrust laws were meant to encourage. It is often extremely difficult, if not impossible, to know where to draw the line. Therefore, if you are a dominant company, are becoming a dominant company, or are an aggressive competitor that is expanding its share of the market, you need to constantly monitor how your company and its employees are conducting themselves in competing with others. That does not mean your company should not attempt to increase its market share or compete aggressively, but it does mean that you should be careful how you do it, because the consequences of not performing properly can be substantial.

### Conspiracy to monopolize

A conspiracy to monopolize requires a concerted action entered into with the specific intent to achieve a monopoly and conduct taken toward that end. Thus, if two or more companies agree to fix prices and there is evidence that they are attempting to monopolize the market through the price-fixing scheme, then a conspiracy to monopolize may be provable.

The requirement of specific intent, as with most other elements in antitrust, can be inferred from the conduct of the parties. The elements needed to prove a conspiracy to monopolize are similar to those needed to prove an attempt to monopolize by a single firm. The difference is that here there is an additional requirement, that is, a conspiracy, whereas there is no requirement of evidence of a "dangerous probability of success." Also, since the conspiracy itself is the act that violates the statutory prohibition against a conspiracy to monopolize, it is not necessary to show that monopoly power was achieved.

As a possibly dominant company in the market, your company would need to make sure that it does not perform in a manner that would be construed similar to conduct prohibited under an attempt to monopolize. In other words, it should not join together or agree with any of its competitors to take action which may be deemed evidence of a conspiracy to monopolize. Joint anticompetitive activity such as price fixing, boycott of competitors, and market allocation may, in addition to being an antitrust violation of itself, be construed as conduct evidencing a conspiracy to monopolize. Remember, no one knows your business as well as you do, and outsiders, including the government enforcement agencies, can work only with the circumstantial evidence they have and draw conclusions from it.

### Shared monopoly

The shared-monopoly theory is that when a few competitors control an industry through their combined market shares (especially an industry with relatively few competitors, for example, an oligopoly) and can keep out other competitors and/or control prices, then such structure and conduct should be a violation of section 2 of the Sherman Act and/or section 5 of the FTC Act. The interdependent conduct, which might include pricing, advertising, dominance of shelf space, brand proliferation, and control of raw materials, should be viewed for possible anticompetitive effects resulting in monopoly power being held by the companies. There is no allegation that the companies are conspiring to monopolize.

The shared-monopoly theory may not fit the traditional

monopoly theories, but it is one means being considered by the government antitrust enforcement agencies to correct an industry structure deemed by the agencies to be anticompetitive. For example, the FTC has brought an action against four producers of ready-to-eat cereal alleging a shared monopoly under section 5 of the FTC Act. As yet there are no cases determining whether the shared-monopoly theory is valid and whether a shared monopoly is violative of either section 2 of the Sherman Act or section 5 of the FTC Act.

### Type of conduct to watch

If you are a dominant factor in your industry or in a particular product line (whether nationally or in some other relevant geographic market area) or are an exceptionally aggressive competitor, you need to consider the possible consequences of your company's conduct in certain areas. Therefore, be careful of the potential elimination of competition or of any particular competitor if or when you:

> Refuse to deal with others.
> Lower prices by a substantial amount.
> Expand a product line.
> Enter new geographic territories.
> "Beef up" advertising campaigns.
> React "aggressively" to a new entry into your market.
> Introduce new market plans, promotions, rebates, discount programs, and similar sales efforts.
> Utilize or demand excessive shelf space.
> Subsidize low prices on a highly competitive product in a competitive area with higher prices and profit margins in other geographic areas or on other product lines.
> Enter into restrictive practices or contracts involving dominant products such as requiring long-term purchase contracts, tying the sale of two products, and exclusive dealing agreements.
> Control the supply of critical ingredients or raw materials.
> Merge or form a joint venture with a strong competitor.

### Defenses

There are certain defenses when a company that does have a monopoly, that is, can control prices or prevent competition, is charged with monopolization.

*The "Thrust-Upon Defense."* The thrust-upon defense is basically that a company holding a monopoly over a particular market for legitimate reasons is not violating the monopolization statute. It may have a monopoly because the demand is so limited that only one company can survive economically, demand is limited by a change in consumer taste, cost of production is too high to retain a large demand and only one company can survive, or one company through its superior skill, foresight, and industry becomes the sole survivor.[4]

*The Natural-Monopoly Defense.* A natural-monopoly defense is based on the fact that the government, at some level, has granted a monopoly position to a company. That includes utilities, public communications, and similar industries and patent holders.

However, even if you have a natural monopoly or a monopoly thrust upon you, you must exercise caution on how you maintain or use it. For example, just because you are a utility does not mean you can automatically assume that you can refuse to wholesale power to competing municipal power systems. A court may find that the refusal, along with other facts, is evidence of an attempt to prevent the establishment of municipal power systems and thereby illegally preserve the company's monopoly.[5]

### Remedies

The remedy for a violation based upon monopolization can vary with each fact pattern. It might include affirmative action such as selling to all customers, sharing critical raw materials, sharing certain know-how or trade secrets, divestiture, dissolution of a particular branch of the company, injunction against certain conduct such as use of distributors, or justifying all price changes.

In addition, treble damages are available to those who were caused injury by the violation, such as competitors driven out of business.

## REFERENCES

1. *United States v. Grinnell Corp.*, 384 U.S. 563 578(1966).
2. *United States v. E.I. du Pont de Nemours & Co.*, 351 U.S. 377(1956).
3. *United States v. Aluminum Co. of America*, 148 F. 2d 416, 424 (2d Cir. 1945).
4. Ibid.; *United States v. United Shoe Machinery Corp.*, 110 F. Supp. 295, 342(D. Mass. 1953), *aff'd. per curiam*, 347 U.S. 521(1954).
5. *Otter Tail Power Co. v. United States*, 410 U.S. 366(1973).

# 8

# Mergers and acquisitions

Because of the complex legal and factual questions that arise in a proposed merger or acquisition, your attorney should be contacted as early as possible before consummation of any such transaction for a review of, among other items, the potential antitrust implications or complications. The attorney will also need to determine whether a "premerger notification" need be filed with the FTC and the Antitrust Division.

A comprehensive review of the law of mergers is beyond the scope of this book. However, the following brief discussion on the application of the antitrust laws to mergers should contribute to your understanding of this area of the antitrust laws and why early consultation with your attorney is important.

The antitrust laws [in particular, section 7 of the Clayton Act, section 5(a)(1) of the FTC Act, and sections 1 and 2 of the Sherman Act] prohibit certain mergers or acquisitions. Section 7 of the Clayton Act, which is the primary statute used to attack mergers, prohibits mergers and acquisitions the effect of which may be to substantially lessen competition, or to tend to create a monopoly. In addition, there are certain procedural requirements of prenotifying the FTC and Antitrust Division before certain mergers or acquisitions are consummated.

The antitrust law on mergers and acquisitions applies whether the transaction involves assets or stock. It can apply to vertical mergers (vertical in the distribution chain), to horizontal mergers (among competitors), and to conglomerate mergers involving nonconnected companies. It can also apply to joint ventures involving entities whose joint venture combination may substantially lessen competition.[1] There are, of course, certain interstate commerce requirements to be met before application of the federal antitrust laws to any merger.

### Antitrust division merger guidelines

The Antitrust Division has merger guidelines[2] that give some indication of where the Division's concern would normally lie, but they have no binding force upon the Division. The FTC has no general guidelines, although it does have guidelines for certain specific industries.[3] The Division's guidelines basically advise what percent of the market held by the two merging companies will trigger an investigation and/or opposition by the Division. In highly concentrated markets wherein the shares of the four largest firms amount to approximately 75 percent or more, the Division will generally question mergers between firms with approximately the following percentages of the market:

| Acquiring Firm, % | Acquired Firm, % |
|:---:|:---:|
| 4 | 4 or more |
| 10 | 2 or more |
| 15 | 1 or more |

When the percentage is not shown, the Antitrust Division suggests interpolation between the nearest percentages that are shown.

In markets of lower concentration, that is, in markets in which the shares of the four largest firms amount to less than approximately 75 percent, the Antitrust Division will generally question mergers between firms accounting for approximately the following percentages of the market:

| Acquiring Firm, % | Acquired Firm, % |
|:---:|:---:|
| 5 | 5 or more |
| 10 | 4 or more |
| 15 | 3 or more |
| 20 | 2 or more |
| 25 | 1 or more |

Again, when a percentage is not shown, the Antitrust Division suggests interpolation between the percentages that are shown.

The Antitrust Division may also challenge mergers that involve less than the above percentages in markets with a trend toward concentration, involve the acquisition of an unusually competitive small company, or involve other factors considered by the Division to effect a substantial lessening of competition.

### Premerger notification rules

The premerger notification rules[4] promulgated by the FTC pursuant to the Hart-Scott-Rodino Antitrust Improvements Act of 1976 are extensive and complex. However, they basically require that the FTC and Antitrust Division be notified of certain acquisitions at least 30 days prior to their consummation. The intent is to give the agencies an opportunity to review the proposed acquisition quickly and determine whether to seek a preliminary injunction to prevent consummation of the transaction if either agency feels the proposed acquisition violates the antitrust laws.

The notification rules apply to domestic and foreign acquisitions and to joint ventures in certain circumstances. The size requirements generally are $100 million in total assets or annual net sales for the acquiring company and $10 million for the company to be acquired. The same size requirements basically apply to joint ventures. There are several exemptions, including one for acquisitions of voting securities if made solely for the purpose of investment and if the acquiring person would end up holding 10 percent or less of the outstanding voting securities of the issuer.

The notification rules require that all studies, surveys, analyses, and reports which were prepared internally or by an outsider for the purpose of evaluating or analyzing the acquisition with respect to market shares, competition, competitors, markets, potential for sales growth, or expansion into product or geographic markets must be submitted to the agencies.

The rules, from time to time, may be amended to some extent to meet the needs and practicalities of compliance. That will be especially true as the FTC gains more experience in implementing them. Therefore, it is important to have your attorney make a determination as to whether any proposed merger involving your company requires premerger notification.

### General questions reviewed in mergers

One of the first questions raised in any merger analysis under the antitrust laws is "what is the relevant market?" As in monopoly cases, the market is determined by defining the product and geographic markets. The market question often becomes the primary area of contention between the parties.

The product market is generally determined by looking at the product in question and any substitutes for that product. Sometimes the courts have said that the substitute products that fall within the product market definition are "determined by the reasonable interchangeability of use or the cross-elasticity of demand between the product itself and substitutes for it."[5] What that means is that each fact situation is unique and the court and parties involved will need to wrestle with what is a factually reasonable and logical product definition while taking into consideration what products are substitutable for what uses, to what extent the products are substitutable for those uses, how the purchasing public views the product and its substitutes, and what factors dictate when a purchaser will buy the product or the questioned substitute.

Thus in looking at the product market the courts sometimes have found a certain "submarket" as the relevant market. To find a relevant submarket within a generally recognized larger market, the courts have used such criteria as industry or public recognition of the particular product market as a separate economic unit, any peculiar characteristics or uses of the product, the need for any unique production facilities, distinct customers, distinct prices (in comparison with other products within the general market), sensitivity to price changes, and specialized vendors. For example, the U.S. Supreme Court has found that within the shoe industry there are relevant submarkets in men's, women's, and children's shoes.[6]

"Geographic market" basically pertains to the "section of the country" within which the effects of the merger would be felt and would possibly substantially lessen competition. Again as with product market, the geographic area that is involved will depend upon the facts of the case and the industry involved. The court may find the significant geographic area to be as small as the Phillipsburg, New Jersey–Eastern Pennsylvania area[7] or as large as the United States, or somewhere in between.

The court will then look at the effect of the merger to determine if competition will be substantially lessened. The result reached by the court will depend upon the facts of the merger, the industry, and the type of merger in question. The type may be horizontal, vertical, or conglomerate.

### Horizontal merger between competitors

A horizontal merger is one between two competitors. Basically, the court will look at the percent of the market that will be held by the merged firm and the amount of concentration that will then be present in the market. It will then determine if such percent of the market and concentration will result or, if the merger is not yet consummated, would result in substantially lessening competition in the market. For example, in *United States v. Von's Grocery,*[8] the Court found that there would be a substantial lessening of competition in the market because the merging of the third and sixth largest retail grocery chains in the Los Angeles metropolitan area would result in the merged company becoming the second largest with 7.5 percent of the market and because the trend in the market was toward a concentration of the retail grocery stores into the larger chains.

Thus in a merger between healthy competitors in a concentrated market or in a market with a trend toward concentration, a small percent of the market as held by the merged company may be sufficient for a court to find a substantial lessening of competition caused by the merger. Naturally, the original question to be answered is what product and geography the market encompasses.

### Vertical merger between supplier and purchaser

A vertical merger is one between two companies in a chain of distribution, that is, supplier and purchaser. The primary concern in reviewing a vertical merger under the antitrust laws is whether the merger forecloses, or may foreclose, a certain percent of the market so that it substantially lessens competition.

A vertical merger can foreclose competition in several ways. It has the potential to foreclose sales by others to the merged customer of the product supplied by the merged supplier. It forecloses competition for the portion of the merged supplier's product that might be "locked up" by the merged customer. It most likely would foreclose the possibility of one of the parties to the merger expanding vertically into the other party's market and thereby becoming a competitor of that party.

That is, if the vertical merger does not occur, then the supplier may begin distributing its product at the same level of the distribution chain as the proposed merged customer or the customer may internally expand its operations to supply that same product and ultimately compete with the proposed merged supplier. For example, if Ford Motor Company were to acquire Autolite, the sparkplug manufacturer, the merger would foreclose the possibility of Ford entering the sparkplug market itself through internal expansion and competing with Autolite for sales to various customers.[9]

Thus, the court will look at the percent of the market

involved, the potential foreclosure as discussed in the paragraph above, the creation of any barriers to entry by new competitors, any trends toward concentration, and related factors pertinent to the particular merger or industry.

## Conglomerate mergers

A conglomerate merger is one between two companies with no direct business relationship. The products of the two companies are not related (such as toys and food products). Conglomerate mergers also include mergers in which the acquiring company is adding a product line complementary or closely related to its present product line, a *product extension merger.* It also includes mergers in which the acquiring company increases its market by acquiring a company that sells the same product but in a different geographic area, a *market extension merger.*

The lessening-of-competition question is more complex when the merger is of the conglomerate type. The percent-of-market-affected test does not apply, since there is no direct effect on a particular market. Therefore, the courts have analyzed conglomerate mergers through a more extensive factual analysis. They generally look at possible reciprocity problems, elimination of potential competition, and creation of barriers to entry.

Reciprocity may arise, for example, when company A acquires company B, which in turn sells to certain customers that sell a particular product to company A. The potential is that company A may require that its suppliers purchase from company B in order to be able to sell to company A.

The elimination of potential competition includes the question whether one of the parties to the merger might have entered the other's market as a competitor were it not for the merger or would have acquired a much smaller company to gain a "toehold" in the particular market. The toehold company, being small, would have given the acquiring company an opportunity to enter the market competitively through the small firm and through use of the acquiring company's added resources.

Another line of reasoning is that the acquiring company, even if it would not have been an actual competitor without the merger, is so positioned on the edge of the market that it would be viewed as a potential competitor by those in the market and would thereby create a favorable influence on the competitive conditions in that market. (An example is the attempted purchase of Clorox by Procter & Gamble.)[10]

The concern for the creation of barriers to entry by a conglomerate merger would arise when the acquiring company has such financial strength or resources that it would create a barrier to most new companies' entering the market. (An example is Procter & Gamble's propensity for heavy financial commitment to advertising.)[11]

### Failing-company defense

In certain limited situations, the "failing-company" defense is available to permit a merger that would otherwise be deemed illegal. Basically, it is that the acquired company is failing, that its resources are so depleted and the prospect of its rehabilitation is so remote that it faces the grave probability of a business failure, and that there is no prospective purchaser for it other than the company attempting to acquire it. Basically, it accepts the situation that all other possibilities have been explored and found to provide no relief and that the sale to the acquiring company is therefore not really damaging to competition—the acquired company would have gone out of the market as a competitor anyway.

### Litigation; tender offers

If a merger is proposed through a tender offer or by negotiated agreement, private plaintiffs or the government may attempt to obtain a preliminary injunction against it pending resolution in the court of the question whether the merger violates the antitrust laws. The preliminary injunction suit itself may last for weeks or months; and if a preliminary injunction is issued, it may require that the companies be held separate even if merged on paper prior to the preliminary injunction.

The preliminary injunction order basically seeks to

maintain the status quo. The standard the plaintiff needs to meet to obtain a preliminary injunction is to show that it has a reasonable probability of success on the merits of the suit and that there is less harm to the defendant companies in preliminarily enjoining the merger than potential harm to the public if the parties do go ahead and merge before the full evidentiary hearing on the merger.

If the plaintiff wins the permanent injunction hearing, it normally obtains a permanent injunction against the merger. If the companies are already merged, it normally requires divestiture after an unscrambling of the two companies. Obviously, the unscrambling is much easier said than done.

Antitrust litigation involving mergers and acquisitions can be, and usually is, very complex, expensive, and time-consuming. In a takeover attempt, it may be too costly for a small firm. It goes without saying that you should bring your attorney in as early as possible when you are considering a merger or acquisition. That will give the attorney an opportunity to review as early as is practical the possible antitrust implications of the proposed merger or acquisition. Thus if there are certain glaring problems, the attorney can let you know immediately. That is some protection against a more costly situation in which the agreement has proceeded toward closing and more time, effort, and money would have to be spent in litigating the matter.

### REFERENCES

1. *United States v. Penn-Olin Chemical Co.,* 378 U.S. 158(1964).
2. 1 CCH Tr. Reg. Rep. par. 4510.
3. 1 CCH Tr. Reg. Rep. par. 4520–4535. The guidelines cover the food distribution industry, dairy industry, and textile mill products industry.
4. 15 U.S.C. sec. 7A; 16 C.F.R. sec. 801 et. seq.
5. *Brown Shoe Co. v. United States,* 370 U.S. 294(1962).
6. Ibid.

7. *United States v. Phillipsburg Natl. Bank & Trust Co.*, 399 U.S. 350(1970).
8. 384 U.S. 270(1966).
9. *Ford Motor Co. v. United States,* 405 U.S. 562(1972).
10. *FTC v. Procter & Gamble Co.*, 386 U.S. 568(1967); see also *United States v. Falstaff Brewing Corp.*, 410 U.S. 526(1973).
11. Ibid.

# 9

# Arrangements involving patents, copyrights, trademarks, and trade secrets

Whether your company is small, medium, or large in size, it is likely to be concerned with trademarks, trade secrets, patents, and/or copyrights at various times. It is thus important to be aware of the applicability of the antitrust laws to such items.

The holder of a patent, copyright, trademark, or trade secret has a natural monopoly. That is not itself illegal under the antitrust laws, but there are situations in which the monopoly privilege can be abused and become conduct that is violative of those laws.

A patent, under the United States patent laws, grants to an inventor of "any new and useful process, machine, manufacture, or composition of matter, or any new and useful improvement thereof"[1] the exclusive right to that invention for a limited term.

A copyright is a legal right given an author to the exclusive right to his writings. It endures for the life of the author and for 50 years after his death.[2]

A trademark generally refers to a name, mark, word, or symbol that identifies the origin and/or manufacture of a product. A trademark may be protected, under certain conditions, through continuous use.

A trade secret (including any know-how information)

may consist of a formula, manufacturing process, device, compilation of information, or the like, which is used in business and which gives the owner an opportunity to obtain an advantage over competitors who do not know or use it. Trade secrets will be protected as long as they are unique and secret.

Obviously, anyone holding a patent, copyright, trademark, or trade secret has a form of a monopoly. The monopoly, generally speaking, is legal as long as it complies with the statutory grant of it. This section assumes, for purposes of discussion (other than for fraud on the patent office), that you have a valid patent, copyright, trademark, or trade secret. The question reviewed here is how to avoid violating the antitrust laws through the use or nonuse of the monopoly.

The purpose of the patent and copyright laws and the philosophy underlying the trademark and trade secret laws have in common the intent to promote invention and creativity which, in theory, will lead to additional economic competition. Thus they are consistent with the purposes of the antitrust laws. However, there can be a parting of the ways when certain conduct would exceed the grant of the legal rights and therefore be violative of the antitrust laws.

Use of a patent, trademark, copyright, or trade secret may involve conduct that falls within the coverage of the antitrust laws and may be considered illegal. Much of the conduct in question would involve some agreement relating to the licensing of one of the rights. The discussion in this chapter will center on patents, but in most situations the same rationale and same results would apply if the right in question were not a patent but a copyright, trademark, or trade secret.

### Licensing of patents

Licensing (that is, a transfer of less than the total rights) is valid unless certain resulting conduct or agreement violates the antitrust laws; that is, certain restrictions contained within a patent-licensing arrangement or abuse of the monopoly rights of a patent may be violative of the antitrust laws.

• If the licensor (patentee) attempts to control the sale price of any products manufactured under the license, the attempt most likely will be deemed violative of the antitrust laws as resale price maintenance. An early U.S. Supreme Court case[3] held that a patentee could dictate prices on such manufactured products; but today that is generally conceded not to be good law, and any such agreement in the license would most likely violate the antitrust laws.

• A patentee is permitted, by statute, to confine an exclusive right to the use of his patent "to the whole or any part of the United States."[4] Therefore, territorial restrictions involving the use of a patent within the United States are generally valid. The limitation is "within the United States," and the statute does not cover any restrictions on territories outside the United States. A patentee can therefore choose how many licensees to have, if any, within the United States and whether to grant exclusive territories.

• Generally, a patentee can control the field of use within which the licensee can sell the item; an example is licensing use of the patent only for the noncommercial field. However, usually the patentee can not include any nonpatented products within a field-of-use restriction.

• Generally, a patentee can control the volume of production of his patented product. However, he can not control the volume of a product produced on a patented machine, because the product is not patented and it is the patented machine that is licensed.

• A license provision that prohibits licensees from dealing in competitive products may be a violation as patent misuse. To determine its validity, a court would take into consideration many of the same factors it would in considering a restriction that prohibits an exclusive distributor from dealing in competitive products. That is, the restriction would fall under the rule-of-reason test.

• The antitrust law relating to tying arrangements involving patents is similar to that in the non-patent area, wherein any requirement that certain patented or nonpatented products be purchased in order to obtain a license to a desired patent is per se illegal. (The assumption is that the other requirements of a tying arrangement be met.) A patent (usually the tying item) is generally presumed to possess the required economic power.

The exceptions or defenses to an otherwise illegal tying arrangement in the non-patent area apply to the patent area also. That is, there is an exception that, when the tied product is not compatible with any product other than the tying product (the patent) or when the patentee's business is new and the patentee has the valid business interest of protecting his future goodwill through requiring the use of certain tied products, then such arrangements may be legal.

• If the license gives certain exclusive territorial rights to the licensee, it is usually permissible for the patentee to also agree not to compete with the licensee within that territory.

• If the patentee agrees to buy all of his needs for certain other products sold by the licensee, the arrangement may be illegal as a reciprocal-dealing agreement.

• The licensing of a package of patents is not itself illegal. However, if you tie one patent to another, the result is a tying arrangement. That form of mandatory package licensing is illegal. Excessively high royalty for only one patent in relation to the royalty for all the patents as a package may be evidence of coercion exercised by the patentee to force the tying arrangement.

• Multiple licensing itself is legal. It may become a violation of the antitrust laws if, for example, there is evidence that the licensees are using it as a vehicle for fixing prices or illegally dividing territories.

• A cross-license agreement is valid. Basically it is the giving of a patent license in exchange for receiving another patent license. The agreement may become suspect, however, if it is between competitors and if the licenses contain some exclusive rights or require approval from the other licensee of some aspect of further licensing.

• A *grant back* is a provision in a patent license which requires the licensee to assign or to license back to the licensor (the original patentee) any improvements made by the licensee on the original patent. It is not illegal, but it comes under the rule-of-reason test. How restrictive is the grant-back provision?

Is it exclusive? Is it available to other competitors? What is the effect upon competition? Did it give the patentee more power in the marketplace to the disadvantage of all others? Is it an improvement needed throughout the industry? Is it part of a scheme to monopolize or to tie in some other product?

## Nonuse of the patent and restrictions on the sale of a patented product

Typically, the nonuse of a patent is permitted, but even it can be abused and violate the antitrust laws. If patentees agree not to use their inventions or discoveries to restrain competition, then there is a per se violation. A violation may also occur if they use their patents to block a new technology or to keep present technology of a competitor within its present state and prevent future competitive advancement of that technology.

Once a patented product is sold, the patentee has no control over it and cannot place restrictions on it, possibly excepting limitations on the field of use, territory, or quantity which are permissible under the patent.

## Fraud on the patent office

If an applicant uses knowing and intentional fraud on the Patent Office to obtain a patent and the patent is used to exclude competition from a relevant market as defined by section 2 of the Sherman Act for monopoly purposes and the other requirements of section 2 are met, then there may be an antitrust violation: an attempt to monopolize. The mere existence of fraud on the Patent Office does not automatically mean there is a violation of the antitrust laws, although there may be a violation of other laws. In order for it to be a violation of the antitrust laws, all of the other elements and conditions of the violation must be met. In other words, it must be shown that the patentee knowingly and willfully misrepresented material facts to the Patent Office.

## Pooling arrangements

A pooling arrangement is an agreement whereby several patentees combine to make available each of their particular patents to other members of the pool. In and of itself the arrangement is not illegal, and in fact it may promote competition by resolving patent conflict arguments, encouraging exchange or availability of blocking patents, and so on. It may be found to be anticompetitive when, for example, the members of the pool are competitors from the same industry and withhold the pooled patents from others. Then the arrangement can be construed as a conspiracy to monopolize, fix prices, allocate territories, or engage in some other anticompetitive activity.

### REFERENCES

1. 35 U.S.C. sec. 101.
2. 17 U.S.C. sec. 302.
3. *United States v. General Electric,* 272 U.S. 476(1926).
4. 35 U.S.C. sec. 261.

# 10.

# Application of
# U.S. antitrust laws
# to international transactions

## General application

Many U.S. firms operate to some extent in the international business arena. That includes participation in foreign distribution agreements or distributor networks; franchise arrangements; license agreements for patent and know-how usage; joint ventures for research, production, and/or distribution; mergers and acquisitions; and various contracts for the sale or purchase of products or raw materials.

The U.S. antitrust laws apply to foreign companies doing business in the United States, at least to the extent to which they apply to U.S. business. In addition, they can apply to international transactions under certain circumstances, and the Department of Justice will and does enforce them in that area. Also, certain private parties, including foreign entities, may have a cause of action arising out of a violation of the U.S. antitrust laws by parties to a particular international agreement or conduct.

As a practical matter, what does that mean? It means that the U.S. antitrust laws have been interpreted by U.S. courts to apply extraterritorially to transactions that would have impact, in some substantial manner, on U.S. foreign trade and commerce (imports and/or exports) through various international transactions. Thus foreign corporations that would agree to restrain U.S. foreign commerce in some manner (as by fixing prices on imports) would be covered, whereas a situation in which U.S. companies joined together strictly for an agreement solely on foreign activities that had no impact on U.S. foreign commerce would, most likely, not be covered.

Often, the real and basic question is whether the U.S. courts have jurisdiction over the parties or over the transaction involved. Even if there is technical jurisdiction, the question that remains is the means available to enforce any judgment obtained by a federal antitrust enforcement agency or a private party. For example, if the defendant company is a foreign corporation with no U.S. assets, any monetary judgment may be difficult to enforce, unless it can be enforced within the foreign country.

The Department of Justice, Antitrust Division, has published a guide to the application of the U.S. antitrust laws to international transactions; it is the *Antitrust Guide for International Operations* (dated January 26, 1977). The *Guide* gives hypothetical cases, discusses the antitrust laws applicable thereto as interpreted by the Antitrust Division, and sets forth their enforcement policy in the antitrust areas covered by the cases.

Several federal antitrust statutes apply to certain international transactions. The Sherman Act applies to activities in or affecting U.S. foreign trade or commerce. Section 3 of the Clayton Act applies to tying arrangements, requirements contracts, and exclusive dealing arrangements that involve "use or consumption, or resale within the United States or any territory under its jurisdiction." Section 7 of the Clayton Act, which covers mergers and acquisitions, most likely includes acquisitions of a foreign company by an American company and covers the acquisition of an American company by a foreign company. The Robinson-Patman Act (price discrimination statute) and FTC Act (unfair methods of competition) also cover certain international transactions.

Thus conduct either in this country or in a foreign country by American and/or foreign companies that in some manner affects U.S. foreign commerce is covered. However, besides the possible difficulty of enforcing a judgment, a problem can be the requirement that it be shown that U.S. foreign commerce was affected. That means that if an agreement, otherwise violative of our federal antitrust laws, is between foreign companies, the acts involved did not take place in the United States, but U.S. foreign commerce was affected, the parties will have violated U.S. antitrust laws.[1]

The breadth of the fact situations that fall within "foreign commerce" has not yet been fully defined by the courts. It is likely that the same types of trade and the same types of conduct will be covered as are covered under domestic application of the antitrust laws through the interstate commerce provision.[2] Thus whatever would be illegal under the federal antitrust laws within the United States most likely would be illegal if it affected foreign commerce.

## Exceptions

There are certain defenses or exceptions that can be raised by private defendants. The U.S. antitrust laws do not, under the *act-of-state doctrine,* apply to acts of foreign governments. Basically, the doctrine is founded on the concept of sovereign immunity, but it does not include activities of the foreign government that would be viewed as commercial rather than governmental in nature.[3] The distinction is obviously a fact question, and it is not always an easy one to make.

The act-of-state doctrine essentially states that our courts cannot question the acts of a foreign government. Thus if a foreign government is involved in anticompetitive conduct, the conduct may be deemed covered by the act-of-state doctrine and thus not considered violative of the U.S. antitrust laws. As an example, a foreign government or one of its agencies might, for political purposes, control a particular entity, operate a state-owned business, or require certain anticompetitive conduct by entities doing business in its country. The act-of-state defense would apply to those actions within the country but not to similar actions taken, or required to be taken, within the United States.

A second defense or exception is identified as *foreign governmental compulsion.* It applies to situations in which certain corporate conduct that would otherwise violate the antitrust laws is required by the government of a foreign country. A company doing business within that country might, for example, be required not to sell to a particular entity or to sell at a certain price. Again, the defense would not cover conduct being required within the United States, nor would mere governmental approval of certain corporate acts provide the foreign governmental compulsion defense. The action must be in response to an order issued as a sovereign in its political domain.

If there are two orders issued by two sovereigns, the United States (through its antitrust laws) and another sovereign, the courts may balance the interests under the *doctrine of comity* and determine which sovereign's interest outweighs the other.

### Application of the substantive law

The U.S. antitrust laws, as developed domestically, would apply to most international transactions in the same way. The analysis, interpretation, and application that would apply to a fact situation within the United States would apply to a similar international situation in which U.S. foreign commerce had been affected. Therefore, generally speaking, a basic understanding of the U.S. antitrust laws will help you analyze potential antitrust concerns in your international transactions.

### Enforcement position of Antitrust Division

The two primary purposes of antitrust enforcement in international commerce, as stated by the Department of Justice, are (1) to protect the American consuming public by assuring it the benefit of competitive products and ideas produced by foreign competitors as well as domestic competitors and (2) to protect

American export and investment opportunities against pri-
vately imposed restrictions.[4]

The *Antitrust Guide for International Operations,* published by the Antitrust Division, sets forth fourteen hypothetical cases involving international transactions of various sorts.
The *Guide* then discusses the cases and often states the Antitrust Division's policy within the particular area. The rest
of this chapter is based on *Guide* comments that relate to
the Antitrust Division's enforcement positions. It will not include the discussion of the cases themselves, because that
discussion, essentially, examines the U.S. antitrust laws as
interpreted in domestic situations and applies the holdings to
international situations. Therefore, if you understand the discussions in other parts of this book on the substantive areas of
the U.S. antitrust laws, you can apply that understanding to
your company's international transactions.

Remember, the following discussion is the Antitrust
Division's enforcement position as reflected in the *Guide,* and
a private party or another enforcement agency would not necessarily take the same view. The discussion is not even binding
upon the Antitrust Division, but it will give you a very good
idea of the Division's position.

## Multinational operation[5]

The Antitrust Division states that it has consistently held that a
parent corporation may allocate territories or set prices for subsidiaries that it fully controls. The Division's test has generally
been whether the parent controls a majority of the voting stock
of the subsidiary or, if the U.S. firm has a minority position,
whether it maintains effective working control. The implication is that the Antitrust Division would view either situation
as one in which the parent controls the subsidiary and may
allocate territories or set prices for the subsidiary.

## U.S. firm's foreign acquisition[6]

Acquisition of a foreign firm that is a major potential entrant in
a U.S. market may be challenged under the U.S. antitrust laws
if the foreign firm is otherwise engaged in U.S. commerce.

Inquiry may be raised if (1) the U.S. market or relevant local market is highly concentrated, (2) the foreign firm is, by virtue of its capability of entering the market, one of a relatively small group of potential entrants, (3) the foreign firm has the incentive to enter the U.S. market, or (4) the foreign firm has the capability of entering the market or threatening to enter. If all those factors are present, the Antitrust Division may take the position that the merger may well violate U.S. antitrust laws regardless of whether, in form, the American firm is acquiring the foreign firm or the foreign firm is acquiring the American firm.

The fact that one firm is of foreign nationality has no special significance under U.S. antitrust law and enforcement policy. The Antitrust Division's enforcement program does not discriminate either against or in favor of business entities on the basis of their citizenship in this or any other antitrust situation. In U.S. antitrust enforcement, it is a firm's role in or its effect upon U.S. commerce that is of concern.

Under an arrangement with member nations of the Organization of Economic Cooperation and Development, the U.S. Government will give notice to a member government of the commencement of an antitrust investigation involving important interests of the member government.

### Joint bidding (joint venture)[7]

An undertaking identified as a "joint venture" is not controlling for antitrust purposes. Instead, antitrust enforcers will be concerned with the reason for a joint venture—and the availability of less anticompetitive alternatives—if the joint venture is among competitors or important potential competitors. The creation of a permanent joint venture will in essence be looked at as if it were a merger between parties in the field covered by the venture.

Normally, the Antitrust Division would not challenge a merger or joint venture whose only effect was to reduce competition among the parties in a foreign market, even when goods or services were being exported from the United States. The rules are even less stringent when a limited, one-shot type of venture that creates a special limited competitor for a special limited purpose is involved. Such short-term consortia are useful when the risks or dollar amounts are large, as in a multiple bank loan or securities underwriting, or when complementary skills are required, as in a typical construction joint venture.

### Joint research (patents)[8]

Whether the Antitrust Division would object to the creation of a research joint venture with a foreign company would depend upon a showing that (1) development costs and risks were high enough to make joint activity appropriate, (2) the venture was not unduly broad in time and scope, and (3) the venturers had continuing competitive incentive from others in the industry to develop the research on an independent basis.

### Manufacturing joint venture and know-how license[9]

If the foreign joint venturer might be a potential entrant into the U.S. market by virtue of its size and/or experience in the field, the joint venture might eliminate potential competition by eliminating the foreign joint venturer as a direct competitor with the U.S. firm in the United States.

If, for example, the U.S. firm had a leading position in a concentrated U.S. market which gave it a substantial degree of market power—the ability to control competitive parameters such as pricing in its market—fear of entry by a firm in the wings of a market may be a significant constraint on its abuse of that power. Therefore, elimination of one very small group of potential entrants could possibly give rise to an antitrust violation. Naturally, further inquiry would be necessary. Whether the foreign joint venturer was capable of developing the product and entering the U.S. market would be significant in determining whether the joint venture would substantially lessen competition.

### Know-how license; tying of license technology[10]

Know-how licensing lacks the protections and legislative mandate of the patent system. Therefore, know-how licenses will, in general, be subject to antitrust standards that are, if anything, stricter than those applied to patent licenses.

In the international context, the presumption against the

legality of a tie-in may not necessarily be as absolute as in the domestic context. In any event, the Antitrust Division may be reluctant to expend resources on international tie-ins which do not have the types of effects on U.S. foreign commerce that it lists as its primary concerns. From the standpoint of U.S. antitrust law, an international tying provision would be of concern if it foreclosed other sellers engaged in U.S. commerce from competing for the tied items. The exclusion of overseas suppliers of the tied items from overseas sales normally would not constitute U.S. foreign commerce, and hence the exclusion is not prohibited by U.S. antitrust law.

The focus of an antitrust inquiry may, therefore, be on whether U.S. exports or imports are possible as a result of a tying arrangement. If they are, no effective exclusion exists. If competing U.S. exports or imports are effectively and unreasonably excluded, the tie-in would appear to violate U.S. antitrust law.

If a U.S. firm's package licensing requirement were imposed upon a foreign customer, the Antitrust Division would be unlikely to seek to invoke U.S. antitrust enforcement jurisdiction unless the requirement had some significant effect on overseas licensing opportunities for other U.S. firms or some impact on sales in the United States.

### Exclusive grant-back licensing[11]

The Antitrust Division has made clear for a number of years that it questions the need for and appropriateness of exclusive grant-back provisions, and it may in an appropriate case wish to assert that an exclusive grant-back requirement involving independent parties is per se illegal. According to the Antitrust Division, exclusive grant-back tends to perpetuate a monopoly of the licensor and may discourage innovation by the licensee. Of course, the licensor has a legitimate interest in assuring that it has access to improvements on its patent, but the Antitrust Division believes that interest can normally be satisfied by a nonexclusive grant back, at least in the case of a nonblocking patent.

Two factors will probably influence the Antitrust Division's decision whether to challenge an exclusive grant back in a particular case. The first concerns the scope of the licensee's obligation to grant back; the second concerns the competitive relations between licensor and licensee.

The relations of the parties may be important for an enforcement decision on an international grant-back obligation. A main thrust of U.S. antitrust enforcement in the international field is to make sure that leading firms do not carve out for themselves broad spheres of territorial and market exclusivity affecting U.S. commerce. An obligation to grant back a U.S. patent or give an exclusive U.S. license to the U.S. licensee may isolate the U.S. market from significant import competition from a leading foreign firm.

A narrowly drawn exclusive grant back in the only license between an American licensor and a foreign single licensee is less serious in competitive effect than the same grant-back clause when it is one of many such arrangements involving the two parties. It is also less serious than when similar clauses are involved in a multiplicity of other licenses from the licensor to other licensees in other countries covering a variety of related areas.

### Exclusive distributorship[12]

The appointment of an exclusive foreign distributor by an American firm does not by itself raise U.S. antitrust concerns. That is essentially a customer-supplier relationship which does not necessarily have a direct impact on either the U.S. domestic market or the export opportunities of other U.S. firms. However, the situation is quite different when both parties to the agreement are substantial manufacturers; for in those circumstances the exclusive distribution agreement creates a territorial allocation between them. Each controls the local sales of its foreign competitor.

If the exclusive arrangement meant not only that the American exporter would not appoint any other distributor in the territory but also that the foreign distributor would not import the goods of any other American manufacturer, then a different case would be presented. It would be relevant whether the foreign distributor were such an important outlet in its own country that the product exclusivity feature of the agreement necessarily restricted in an important way the ability of other American firms to export to that market. Inquiry would cover (1) whether it was illegal under foreign law or was commercially impossible for the distributor to handle competing U.S. products or (2) whether any less restrictive alternative was available.

A safer course would be for the parties to appoint someone other than a competing manufacturer as an exclusive foreign distributor. When a foreign manufacturer is used, the Antitrust Division will look with particular care at the impact on U.S. commerce. It is especially important that significant foreign products which could compete in U.S. markets not be confined to exclusive channels for distribution dominated by a directly competing U.S. manufacturer already well established in the field.

### Price stabilization by a foreign country[13]

If a foreign country requires a U.S. firm that is doing business within that country and exports a product from that country to the United States to sell that product at a specified price within the United States, the government itself may be immune from antitrust liability as a foreign sovereign but its immunity does not shield the distributor for its activities in the United States. Nor may the distributor avail itself of the act-of-state or foreign-compulsion defense. Here the government-directed conduct is within the United States, and not within the foreign country.

The Antitrust Division believes the United States antitrust laws represent a fundamental and important national policy. In this case, the purpose and necessary effect of a foreign country's "command"—to create a per se antitrust violation in the U.S. market—is contrary to that policy. Accordingly, the Division does not believe comity would require that the United States treat the foreign country's command as controlling here.

### Dealing with a cartel; political risk insurance[14]

A situation in which a foreign government is involved through partial or complete ownership or control of a company participating in a cartel, or the country itself is participating in a cartel to determine quotas and prices for products that would be exported into the United States or sold to foreign brokers who would resell a portion into the United States, would be a clear violation under the U.S. antitrust laws. That is true unless defenses peculiar to the international situation apply to particular defendants.

The act-of-state doctrine, foreign-compulsion doctrine, and comity would need to be determined. Those defenses may not be available to the private parties involved in the cartel. The next question would be whether the U.S. courts could obtain jurisdiction over the private parties. The assumption is that comity does not dictate that the Antitrust Division not enforce the U.S. antitrust laws against the private party participants.

The act-of-state doctrine does not apply to commercial actions of a foreign government or instrumentality; it applies to public, political actions. Therefore, a factual determination must be made. A valid decree of a foreign government usually would meet the requirement of a public state action. The fact that one of the companies apparently was controlled by a foreign government would not provide the company with an act-of-state defense in a U.S. antitrust action. The act-of-state defense does not extend to "commercial" activities of a foreign country or of a business corporation partially or wholly owned by a foreign country.

### Government-imposed restraint[15]

A situation in which a U.S. company or its foreign subsidiary joined with other competitors in a foreign country to suggest that either a tariff increase or an embargo be legislated for a specified period for particular products would raise Noerr-Pennington questions if the legislative action affected exports by other U.S. firms into the foreign country. The key restraint on the U.S. export competition would have been imposed by the foreign government. The only question, therefore, would be whether the Noerr-Pennington doctrine applied to efforts to cause a foreign government to impose restraints on U.S. commerce. The Antitrust Division does not consider the Noerr-

Pennington doctrine to be limited to the domestic area. Therefore, the activity might be protected under the Noerr-Pennington doctrine. [See Petitioning the Government (Noerr-
Pennington Doctrine), Chapter 12.]

## Foreign antitrust laws

There may be antitrust laws in effect in the foreign country in
which you are doing business. What they prohibit and how
they have been interpreted depends upon the particular set of
laws. For example, the European Common Market has certain
antitrust laws which it enforces. To do business within the
Market would dictate that your company be aware of at least
the general nature of those provisions.

### REFERENCES

1. *United States v. Aluminum Co. of America,* 148 F. 2d 416 (2d Cir.
   1945).
2. ABA, *Antitrust Law Developments,* 359(1975).
3. *Alfred Dunhill, Inc. v. Republic of Cuba,* 425 U.S. 682(1976);
   Foreign Sovereign Immunities Act of 1976, 28 U.S. at secs. 1602
   et. seq.
4. U.S. Department of Justice, *Antitrust Guide for International Operations,* January 26, 1977, pp. 4 and 5.
5. Ibid., pp. 10–14.
6. Ibid., pp. 15–18.
7. Ibid., pp. 19–22.
8. Ibid., pp. 23–27.
9. Ibid., pp. 28–32.
10. Ibid., pp. 33–39.
11. Ibid., pp. 42–45.
12. Ibid., pp. 46–49.
13. Ibid., pp. 50–52.
14. Ibid., pp. 53–61.
15. Ibid., pp. 62–63.

# 11

# Government enforcement of the antitrust laws

The federal antitrust laws are enforced by the Antitrust Division of the Department of Justice and by the Federal Trade Commission. The state antitrust laws are generally enforced by the state attorney general's offices, but some state statutes provide for enforcement by additional agencies. For example, the Ohio and California antitrust statutes provide for enforcement not only by the state attorneys general but also by county prosecutors (Ohio) and local district attorneys (California).

This chapter will discuss government enforcement agencies, their role in enforcing the various statutes, their investigative authority, how they determine what conduct or companies should be investigated, and how to deal with the enforcement agency during an investigation.

## United States Department of Justice, Antitrust Division

The Antitrust Division has responsibility for criminal and civil enforcement of the Sherman and Clayton Acts. (The Federal Trade Commission also has responsibility for enforcement of the Clayton Act.) In addition to its main office in Washington, D.C., the Antitrust Division has field offices in Atlanta, Chicago, Cleveland, Dallas, Los Angeles, New York, Philadelphia, and San Francisco. Each field office has jurisdiction over a specific geographic area (see Appendix B), but the Washington office may be involved in matters anywhere in the country. Once in a while a field office may be involved in a suit outside its assigned geographic territory, but generally each office concentrates upon its own area.

The Antitrust Division has over 400 attorneys, a staff of economists, and supporting personnel in its Washington, D.C. and field offices. It is headed by an Assistant Attorney General who is appointed by the President. Usually there are three deputy assistant attorneys general who have overall supervisory responsibility for different aspects of the Division including overseeing the eight field offices. The various field offices and certain sections of the Washington, D.C. office investigate possible antitrust violations and litigate alleged antitrust violations.

The Antitrust Division has authority to investigate both possible criminal and civil violations, and it can file a criminal and/or civil suit arising out of a particular antitrust investigation. The Division generally will file a criminal action only involving per se offenses. (See the discussion of "per se" in Chapter 3.) Generally, the criminal actions have consisted of various price-fixing cases, bid rigging (considered a form of price fixing), horizontal refusals to deal (sometimes referred to as boycotts or blacklisting), horizontal division of territories or allocation of customers, and vertical resale price fixing.

However, the Antitrust Division could, at least theoretically, file a criminal suit for any violation of the Sherman Act such as a vertical agreement on exclusive distributor territory the effect of which is now looked at under the rule-of-reason test. The position of the Antitrust Division is that it will bring criminal action only when the defendant was put on notice through an identification of certain activities as per se illegal or the public has been put on notice that certain activity will be attacked with a criminal indictment.

Usually when it files a criminal suit, the Antitrust Division will file a companion civil suit seeking an injunction to prohibit the conduct under attack from occurring in the future. It may also file a separate civil suit seeking damages suffered by the United States as a result of the alleged conduct. (For example, the government might suffer damages from the purchase of a certain quantity of a product the price of which has allegedly been fixed.) Sometimes the civil damage suit will also make a claim under the False Claims Act. Under the federal antitrust laws the United States can seek only single damages (actual damages) and not the treble damages that can be claimed by private plaintiffs. (The term "private plaintiffs" does include such other government entities as states and municipalities.)

### Investigative procedure and authority

*Sources of Information to Initiate an Investigation.* How does the Antitrust Division uncover violations? By luck and hard work. It initiates investigations and inquiries as the result of complaints filed by customers, suppliers, competitors, and consumers. It may also be prompted to take the initiative by news articles, economic studies, or voluntary confessions. There is nothing mysterious about how an investigation is begun or is called to the attention of the Antitrust Division. In fact, you may seriously consider contacting the Division or some other government antitrust enforcement agency to provide information of a possible violation. The situation may be one that is damaging your competitive position; and rather than proceed directly through litigation, you may choose to notify a government enforcement agency in the hope that the agency will proceed against the alleged violators.

Sometimes the Antitrust Division receives a request from Congress or information from another government agency and then investigates the conduct in question. It also receives identical bid information on purchases or sales exceeding $10,000 by a department, agency, or instrumentality of the government when that entity has received two or more identical bids, including bids that are identical after discounts.[1]

The Antitrust Division has a staff of economists who

assist in the initial review of conduct in question, again in any later investigation, and during litigation. For example, in reviewing certain pricing conduct, an economist might conduct economic surveys of pricing patterns of a particular product or industry, possibly in a particular geographic area. He would take into consideration whether the product was fungible, whether labor costs and other costs were standard, whether there were any cost variables, the supply and demand, and other relevant factors. He would then determine the likely outcome based on that information and use it as a measure against the actual pricing pattern of the particular product or industry.

Another example might be an investigation of sealed bids for supplying a particular product to certain governmental institutions. The economist would review the pattern of those bids, that is, which companies submitted bids to which agencies and what the bid prices were to each agency. He would then determine whether, from an economist's standpoint, the bid patterns indicate that there must have been an agreement to predetermine the prices and/or allocate the bids among the different agencies.

*Informal Investigation.* The Antitrust Division will often initiate an investigation by use of the Federal Bureau of Investigation, Antitrust Division attorneys either in person or by letter of inquiry, or by a combination of those informal contacts. It may contact and attempt to interview or obtain information from anyone who filed a complaint and from customers, suppliers, and competitors of any company(s) or person(s) under investigation. At this stage, you have no legal requirement to answer any questions asked or to turn over any documents requested. Before you do anything, you should contact your attorney. Advise the FBI or Antitrust Division attorney that you want to do that. Get the name, business card, and phone number of the FBI agent or Antitrust Division attorney, the area of your business that the agent or attorney wants to question you about, the documents he wants, and generally what he is interested in and any other information that you can obtain. Provide all that information to your attorney.

It may be in your and your company's interest to cooperate voluntarily. Your company may not be a target of the investigation, and you might be able to convince the government agents that you and your company are not involved. You may be able to explain away any apparent questionable activity. To make that decision, you need time to think, cogitate, and discuss the possible ramifications.

Before you give an interview (after talking with your attorney, and preferably with your attorney present), request that you be furnished a copy of any recordation of it. The Antitrust Division attorney will generally agree and provide you with a recordation, but the FBI generally will not.

Pay attention to letters received from any of your customers, suppliers, franchisees, or distributors accusing you or your company of an antitrust violation. You may be able to resolve the matter amicably between the parties or even explain in a convincing manner to the complainant that there is no antitrust violation. Otherwise, a letter of that type may end up with the Antitrust Division and initiate an investigation of your company.

If you do provide information in the form of interviews, documents, or both, do not provide false information; to do so could lead to criminal sanctions: a fine of up to $10,000 and/or imprisonment up to 5 years.[2] Likewise, once you have been contacted in connection with an investigation, do not attempt to destroy any documents that may be relevant to the investigation. That too can result in a fine and/or imprisonment.

As part of the mechanics of providing documents to the Antitrust Division, make sure that you keep a copy, preferably the original, and provide the Division with a copy. Make a record of which documents you turn over to the Division. If the investigation goes further than an informal stage, that information will be extremely helpful to your attorney in determining exactly what the Division has.

### Criminal investigation through use of a grand jury

The Antitrust Division can conduct an investigation of a potential criminal antitrust violation through use of the grand jury. However, it is not permitted to use the grand jury solely to obtain information for use in a civil antitrust case. Grand jury proceedings are held in secret, and witnesses may not be accompanied by their attorneys in the grand jury room itself. However, a witness is permitted to leave the grand jury room to consult with his attorney about particular areas or questions that arise during the grand jury questioning.

Generally, a witness can discuss with others what transpired in the grand jury room. In other words, there is nothing to prevent a witness from disclosing what went on in the grand jury room. However, the disclosure may have adverse consequences for the witness or the company during a civil treble damage trial involving the particular antitrust conduct under investigation. For example, if a witness voluntarily discusses the questions and his answers in the grand jury, he may be required to answer those questions again outside the secrecy of the grand jury, any recipient of the conversation may be required to testify as to what was said by the witness, or the witness' grand jury testimony transcript might be ordered released to the other parties.

Therefore, if you are a witness before a grand jury, discuss nothing concerning the grand jury with anyone until you consult with your attorney to determine the potential risk of the discussion and whether the risk is balanced by other factors. That is not to say that a witness should not discuss the results of the grand jury appearance with his attorney or with the attorney for his company. Generally, such a conversation is privileged under the attorney-client relation or work product doctrine. (Even that, however, may not be sufficient to keep the information from being revealed at a later time by order of the court.)

The grand jury has rather broad powers by which it can subpoena documents or the testimony of an individual or a representative of a corporation. If the Antitrust Division has reason to believe that the document request has not been complied with fully, it may take one of two actions. It may subpoena the person in charge of the search for the documents, or it may seek a search warrant to examine the documents themselves to determine whether your company is in compliance with the subpoena.

Sometimes a court in a later civil treble damage action based upon the allegation of a criminal indictment will permit a release of grand jury testimony and/or the turning over of documents provided to the grand jury in its investigation of the particular antitrust concern. When the court will release the testimony and/or documents, if at all, depends upon many factors, including a subjective determination by the judge.

Your company may be required, whether or not it is under investigation by the grand jury, to provide certain documents requested by the subpoena. It may also be required to provide an employee familiar with a specifically identified aspect of your company or its business to testify before the grand jury. Such testimony can also be sought from specifically identified individuals.

Whenever a grand jury subpoena is received, it means the grand jury is looking into a possible criminal violation. The subpoena will, in general terms, identify the type of conduct and the statute in question. Just because you or your company receives a subpoena does not necessarily mean that you are or it is a potential target of the investigation. But you and your company are entitled to full constitutional rights, and you should contact your attorney immediately. To do so will provide your attorney with valuable time within which to attempt to contact the Antitrust Division, assist you in accumulating documents, investigate the matter internally on your behalf, and take whatever steps are necessary for proper representation of you and/or your company.

There are certain obligations that you and your company must meet in the event of a subpoena. Ignoring a grand jury subpoena can cause you and/or your company to be held in contempt of court. Lying to the grand jury, destroying documents, telling half-truths, or supplying only part of the documents subpoenaed can result in criminal sanctions of a fine and/or jail sentence. Even your normal record destruction policy must be stayed as it applies to documents possibly covered by a subpoena. The same obligation exists when a suit has been filed.

Individuals are protected against self-incrimination, including the right not to testify before a grand jury. Since there is a risk of unwittingly waiving that right, early contact with your attorney can be crucial. There are other constitutional and statutory rights to which you and/or your company are entitled. They can be adequately identified only by your attorney as applicable to the particular situation.

The Antitrust Division takes the position that if an individual employee and his company become the target of a grand jury investigation, then the two should have separate counsel. The Division feels that the interests of the individual and the company may not always be compatible, which would put an attorney who was attempting joint representation in the position of potential or actual conflict of interest.

### Civil antitrust investigation; use of civil investigative demands

In investigating a possible antitrust violation that might result in a civil antitrust suit, the Antitrust Division has broad investigative authority. It includes the use of subpoenas to obtain testimony, documents, and responses to written questions from natural, as well as corporate, persons; from third parties; and from persons under investigation, as long as the Division has reason to believe that such persons have information relevant to the investigation.[3] It permits the Division to seek information and documents in anticipation of a proposed merger, acquisition, joint venture, or similar arrangement and to investigate present or past conduct that may involve most other alleged antitrust violations.

There are, however, certain limitations on the scope of the civil investigative demands (CID), and there are certain rights the recipient can exercise. For example, the CID's must state the nature of the conduct constituting the alleged violation, and the request for documents must be stated with "definiteness and certainty." In addition, the CID's are subject to certain other standards such as objections on the grounds of relevance, burdensomeness, attorney-client privilege, and work product privilege. Persons who would give testimony in a deposition as a result of being subpoenaed through a CID may refuse to answer questions on the grounds of possible self-incrimination or any other constitutional or legal right or privilege.

At all stages of the investigation, the individual and/or the company may have his or its attorney present to advise and, when appropriate, to object to certain questioning. Therefore, upon receipt of a CID, you or your company should immediately contact your attorney to discuss all of the ramifications of the CID and the posture that you or your company should take.

You need to be aware that there may be criminal sanctions if a CID recipient intentionally gives, or attempts to give, false information or documents or attempts to avoid compliance with the CID other than through legal procedures. That would include withholding information or documents, misrepresenting, destroying, altering, concealing, or in any other manner not complying with the subpoena and the questions asked other than through legal procedure. The sanctions could be a fine up to $5,000 and/or 5 years in prison.

Thus, through a CID, your company may be required to provide an employee to be deposed or the CID may specifically identify a particular individual to be deposed. In addition, even though your company may not be under investigation, it may receive a subpoena for documents or testimony which you will be required to produce.

Often, when you have received a CID or a grand jury subpoena for documents, you can contact the Antitrust Division attorney responsible and discuss the possibility of modifying the subpoena to permit you to comply on a less burdensome basis and still provide the type of documents sought. Antitrust Division subpoenas are often issued in a very broad manner, since Division personnel do not have your perspective of your industry and records. Often they will be cooperative in attempting to resolve any overreaching or wide breadth of the subpoena. If not, there is the possibility of your company's going into court in an attempt to obtain a court order prohibiting the total production of documents as sought by the CID. This may or may not be successful, as courts typically are very liberal in permitting and requiring compliance with CID's (as well as grand jury subpoenas and subpoenas in private litigation, including antitrust litigation).

### Coordination with other enforcement agencies

The Antitrust Division will usually coordinate its major investigations with the Federal Trade Commission. In fact, each agency has representatives that meet with representatives of the other agency to discuss potential investigations, determine whether there may be an overlap, and so avoid duplicate investigations. In addition, the Antitrust Division is permitted to turn over to the Federal Trade Commission and to Congress any information obtained through the use of CID's. The FTC is subject to the same restrictions as govern the use of the information by the Department of Justice: any information obtained can be used as evidence only in a judicial or administrative proceeding.

Whenever the Attorney General has brought an action under the antitrust laws, most likely through the Antitrust Division, and he has reason to believe that a state attorney general would be entitled to bring an action under the federal antitrust laws based substantially on the same alleged violation, he is obliged by federal antitrust laws to give prompt written notification to the state attorney general. To the extent permitted by law, and upon the request of the state attorney general, the Antitrust Division will make available to the state official any investigation files or other materials which are or may be relevant or material to the actual or potential federal antitrust cause of action.

The files and other material are intended to assist the state attorney general in evaluating the potential federal antitrust cause of action, but it is unclear exactly what information can and can not be revealed. However, it is likely that any information obtained through a CID would not be subject to being revealed under the federal statute. In addition, if a grand jury investigation is ongoing or a resulting criminal suit has not yet been resolved, the Antitrust Division would resist a request by a state to turn that information over prior to resolution of the criminal indictments.

Ultimately, a transmission would most likely depend upon the court's findings as to the need to keep the grand jury secrecy and the court's interpretation of the statute. Thus it is possible that information you provide to the Antitrust Division may be turned over, and in fact the U.S. Attorney General may be required to turn it over to a state attorney general.

### Resolution of investigations without litigation

Sometimes an investigation by the Antitrust Division will result in no further inquiry by the Division. It is possible that the initial inquiry or subsequent inquiries will not provide evidence sufficient to support an antitrust violation allegation or will provide evidence that no violation involving the conduct in question exists. The same thing may be true of information provided to a grand jury, with the result that the jury will not issue any indictments or will not issue indictments against particular individuals or companies while issuing them against others.

In a civil investigation you may be able to reach some form of compromise or settlement before litigation. It may take the form of a letter of assurance by your company that it will not engage in certain conduct or an agreed court order assuring the same thing. However, a resolution through that form of settlement is not too common.

Sometimes through cooperation with and assistance to the Antitrust Division your company may relieve itself of future litigation to resolve the same issues. (The same is true of an investigation conducted by the Federal Trade Commission.) However, substantial risk is involved in unbridled cooperation and assistance. You need to discuss the risks versus the potential benefits with your attorney prior to any discussions with the Antitrust Division or the turning over to or the review by the Division of any documents.

### Resolution of criminal litigation

If a criminal indictment is filed against you or your company, then you and it have several initial alternatives: to plead guilty, to plead not guilty, or to be permitted to plead nolo contendere.

If you plead guilty, then the matter is resolved as to involvement in the alleged antitrust violation and the next steps will be a probation report to investigate your background, your company's background, other violations, and other pertinent information for the judge to review prior to sentencing. The Antitrust Division has issued *Guidelines for Sentencing Recommendations* which sets out the Division's position on sentences. The *Guidelines* recommend a basic sentence of 18 months for individuals and a minimum fine of $100,000 for corporations, to be adjusted upward or downward depending upon various listed factors.

If the plea is not guilty, then the various discovery procedures will occur prior to the criminal trial. You and your attorney will be engaged in lengthy preparation to prove your innocence at trial.

A plea of nolo contendere is a plea of no contest; that is, you do not admit nor do you deny the allegations of the indictment. For most purposes a nolo contendere plea is considered a plea of guilty by the court and by the federal statutes. After a nolo contendere plea is entered, the court sentences the individual or company. Both for guilty pleas and for nolo contendere pleas a company is subject to a fine up to $1 million and an individual is subject to a fine up to $100,000 and imprisonment up to 3 years or both. However, whether you can enter a nolo plea is discretionary with the judge. Some judges will not accept a nolo plea, and the Antitrust Division will often oppose acceptance.

There is one important distinction between a guilty plea and a nolo contendere plea under the federal antitrust laws. A private antitrust plaintiff who alleges the same antitrust violation as encompassed within the criminal indictment can use the guilty plea as prima facie evidence that the allegations of the antitrust violation are true. A nolo contendere plea, on the other hand, cannot be used as prima facie evidence of violation. (See Prima Facie Case, Chapter 3.)

If the prima facie rule is in effect, then the burden in a private civil action shifts immediately from the plaintiff being required to prove the antitrust violations to the defendant being required to disprove that the violations exist. In other words, the defendant was not prohibited from disputing the finding of the antitrust violations but now has the burden of disproving the finding. In most circumstances, disproving the presumption of violation would be extremely difficult.

If the criminal case goes to trial, it is tried in a U.S. District Court before a jury, unless the jury is waived. The rulings and finding, if it is of guilt, can be appealed to the U.S. Circuit Court of Appeals and then ultimately to the U.S. Supreme Court if the Court accepts the appeal.

### Resolution of civil enforcement litigation

If the Antitrust Division files a civil antitrust enforcement suit (sometimes in conjunction with a criminal indictment), then you have two possible courses of action. The first is to litigate, and the second is to attempt to work out a consent decree (consent judgment) with the Antitrust Division and thereby resolve the conflict.

A consent decree is an agreed-upon judgment whereby both parties agree, and the court order provides, that certain conduct will not transpire in the future. The defendant neither admits nor denies that it ever engaged in that conduct. The consent decree typically will include provisions for annual reporting to the Antitrust Division, the right of the Division to review books and records during normal business hours to determine whether there has been compliance with the consent decree, and any other provisions deemed necessary or appropriate to obtain compliance with the consent decree and prevent the conduct being prohibited.

If the civil allegations are such as an attempt to monopolize or certain other litigation that seeks to substantially alter a method of distribution or position within the industry, the proposed consent decree most likely will seek much of the same relief as if the Antitrust Division had won the litigation.

A consent decree is not considered prima facie evidence against you in a private treble damage action, since you are not admitting any violation of the antitrust laws. If, on the other hand, you litigate and lose the civil action, then the finding of a violation is prima facie evidence of the antitrust violation in a later private treble damage action. However, you do not have a right to enter into a consent decree, and you may be forced to litigate if the Antitrust Division refuses to accept it.

Once a consent decree is finalized between the government and the defendant, it must be published in the *Federal Register* along with an explanation (called an impact statement) of why the Antitrust Division entered into the consent decree rather than litigate the matter. Comments are invited. After 60 days the consent decree and any comments are filed with the court for final acceptance of the consent decree and make the decree an order of the court.

### Resolution of government damage action

The resolution of an action filed by the Antitrust Division for damages to the United States because of an alleged antitrust violation committed by your company and possibly other defendants presents you with two basic choices: litigate or attempt to resolve the matter through a settlement.

A federal government antitrust damage action does not give rise to the prima facie evidence rule because it is not an enforcement action. However, as a practical matter, if you were to litigate and lose the lawsuit and private treble damage plaintiffs had similar suits alleging the same basic facts pending against you, an argument called *collateral estoppel* could be presented to use the findings of the related cases. Whether the court would permit the use would depend upon the facts surrounding the particular litigation.

The other means of resolution is the settlement of the damage claim by the United States. Settlement would occur in the same manner as the resolution of any other damage claim between two private litigants; that is, there are no unusual ramifications or risks when the United States is the plaintiff seeking damages under the antitrust laws. The only difference is that the antitrust laws prohibit the United States from seeking treble damages and specifically limit the United States to seeking its actual damages suffered as a result of the alleged antitrust violation.

### Business review procedure

The Antitrust Division has set up the *business review procedure,* whereby a business can request it to state its enforcement intentions upon a prescribed set of facts. The procedure does not require the Division to state its position, but it does provide an opportunity for it to state its position upon request. If it does state a position in response to the request, it will do so only as of the date of the statement. That is, the Division will not make a statement that will bind it in the future in relation to the same or a similar set of facts.

The Division reserves the right to request additional facts and documents when a business review letter is sought. It also reserves the right to use any information it receives in any enforcement proceeding. A request for a business review letter must be made in writing, and it can ask for review only of *proposed* business conduct. The Antitrust Division will review possible criminal actions, but it will not usually give its position on civil actions other than on mergers and acquisitions.

The requesting party must submit all relevant facts and data including copies of any pertinent documents. The Antitrust Division may then ask for further information and/or documents and/or conduct its own investigation. It is at this point that it will decide whether to state or decline to state its enforcement intentions.

Thirty days later the Antitrust Division puts all the information and documents on file and makes them available to the public. An applicant can request confidentiality of the information and documents provided it can show that the information, if made public, would have a detrimental effect on its business.

The advantage in obtaining a business review letter is to know beforehand what the position of the Antitrust Division will be. The disadvantage, of course, is that you provide the Antitrust Division with possible evidence to be used against you. Also, unless your request for confidentiality is granted, the information will eventually be available to the public.

### How to register an antitrust complaint with the Antitrust Division

If you suspect that you have been a victim of an antitrust violation, you can contact the Antitrust Division and call the conduct to its attention. (Of course, you could also complain to the FTC and/or the antitrust section of the state attorney general's office.) Consider contacting the regional office responsible for your area. (See Appendix B.) You can also register your complaint with the Washington office. You may wish to discuss the matter with your attorney to frame any written complaint properly.

Whether you contact the FTC, the Antitrust Division, or the state attorney general is discretionary. Sometimes one agency will refer a matter to another if it feels the other agency is the more likely one to handle the complaint. If the complaint involves price fixing or horizontal allocation of markets, the Antitrust Division, with its criminal enforcement authority, may obtain more effective results. For other possible violations, which agency is more likely to pursue the complaint may depend upon the industry. If you are, or your attorney is, aware of a particular agency investigating the industry within which your complaint falls, then that agency should be contacted.

You may want to contact several agencies. Sometimes one agency is not interested in pursuing a particular complaint for any number of reasons, including lack of resources and the whim of the person reviewing your complaint, whereas another agency will be interested. Sometimes it takes a while to investigate, even preliminarily, so that you may not be aware of any activity on the part of the agency for a long period of time, if ever.

The more information you can provide, the more likely an agency will be interested. A suspicion, coincidence, or isolated act is not usually going to create much interest or concern. If there is strong evidence of a potential antitrust violation, there will be interest. In addition, sometimes complaints from various sources can help the agency to piece together evidence of a possible violation. And in all honesty, sometimes the enforcement agencies receive misleading or irrelevant complaints from disgruntled ex-employees, unsuccessful competitors, and unsatisfied customers.

If no response is obtained, either you or your attorney can ask for the status of your complaint. You may or may not get a status report from the Antitrust Division. Often the Division will neither admit nor deny that it is proceeding with any complaint. Remember, if the United States brings a suit for enforcement of the federal antitrust laws and the court or jury finds the defendants in violation, the finding will be prima facie evidence against the same defendants for that particular conduct in any private treble damage suit by anyone (including your own company) injured by that conduct.

### Policy of self-confession

The Antitrust Division has an announced policy of self-confession. That is, if a company and/or employee voluntarily goes to the Division and "confesses" an antitrust violation, the Division may be lenient in prosecution of the violation against that company or individual. Leniency apparently would include the possibility of not being criminally indicted or civilly sued.

The Antitrust Division has indicated that it still reserves its traditional prosecutorial discretion and that leniency will not be automatic. Factors that are taken into consideration include whether the individual or business is the first to come forward, whether the confession is truly that from a corporation rather than merely an individual, whether the Antitrust Division could reasonably have expected to become aware of the antitrust violation even if not brought to its attention, whether the company immediately attempted to cease the conduct in question once it became known to the company, the amount of openness and thoroughness with which the company presents the information to the Antitrust Division, and whether the company expects and offers to make restitution to any of the injured parties.[4]

## The Federal Trade Commission

The Federal Trade Commission was created by Congress in 1914; today it has the obligation to enforce the Federal Trade Commission Act and, in conjunction with the Department of Justice, the Clayton Act. It also enforces the Fair Packaging and Labeling Act, the Wool Products Labeling Act of 1939, the Fur Products Labeling Act, the Textile Fiber Products Identification Act, the Truth in Lending Act, the Fair Credit Reporting Act, and the Magnuson-Moss Act.

The FTC does not have criminal enforcement authority. Only the Antitrust Division of the Department of Justice has such authority, and that is to enforce the Sherman Act and section 3 of the Robinson-Patman Act. The staff of the Federal Trade Commission consists of approximately 300 to 400 attorneys, a number of economists, and supporting personnel.

Section 5(a)(1) of the FTC Act states that "unfair methods of competition in or affecting commerce, and unfair or deceptive acts or practices in or affecting commerce, are hereby declared unlawful." As you can see, the language is extremely broad, and it has been subject to interpretation over the years by various courts in various cases. The phrase "unfair methods of competition" is the portion of section 5(a)(1) that applies to antitrust violations, and "unfair or deceptive acts or practices" relates basically to consumer protection enforcement activities by the FTC. As it applies to anticompetitive conduct, section 5(a)(1) has been given very broad interpretation by the courts. It includes any activity normally covered by most of the other federal antitrust statutes, as well as activity that would have a "tendency" to be anticompetitive rather than presently being or having been anticompetitive.

## Structure of the FTC

The enforcement section of the Commission is divided into the Bureau of Competition and the Bureau of Consumer Protection. The two bureaus are supported by the Bureau of Economics, which supplies the Commission itself and the enforcement bureaus with economic expertise, advice, data, surveys, and reports.

The Bureau of Competition is headed by a director who has a staff and whose assistant directors head various groups within the Bureau's hierarchy. The Bureau of Competition is divided into various sections which investigate and litigate the alleged antitrust violations that come within the responsibility of the Federal Trade Commission. It has regional offices in Atlanta, Boston, Chicago, Cleveland, Dallas, Kansas City, Los Angeles, New Orleans, New York, San Francisco, and Seattle in addition to its main headquarters in Washington, D.C., which has national responsibility. Each of the regional offices has an assigned territory. (See Appendix B.) Like the Antitrust Division, the Bureau of Competition attempts to coordinate the efforts of the regional offices and the Washington office, and it will assign one or the other to investigate and litigate alleged antitrust violations within a particular area.

The Bureau of Competition does not litigate its suits in a United States district court as the Antitrust Division does; instead, the FTC has administrative law judges for the purpose. A ruling by an administrative law judge can be appealed to the FTC, and the commission's decision can be appealed to the U.S. Circuit Court of Appeals. Ultimately, a request (petition for certiorari) can be made to the U.S. Supreme Court to hear an appeal from the Court of Appeals.

The FTC consists of five commissioners appointed by the President with the advice and consent of the Senate. The commissioners have staggered terms of 7 years, and no more than three commissioners may be from the same political party. As mentioned above, the Commission hears appeals from an administrative law judge's decision. The Commission can make its own factual as well as legal determinations on the issues.

The Commission also issues industry guides, trade regulation rules, and advisory opinions. They are discussed later in this chapter.

### Investigative procedure and authority

Under the FTC Act, the Commission is given power to "make rules and regulations for the purpose of carrying out the provisions" of the Act. Under that authority, the Commission has implemented the various rules and procedures for the conduct of its day-to-day activities and the procedures for investigation, adjudication, and rule making (industry guides, trade regulation rules, and advisory opinions).

The FTC has been given broad investigatory powers. They include the power to require corporations to file annual or special reports and to answer specific questions whether or not the FTC is conducting an investigation of the particular corporation. In other words, in addition to the power to conduct an investigation of a possible antitrust violation, the FTC also has the power to compile economic studies and reports to determine whether particular industries or types of conduct should be investigated for possible violation of the antitrust laws that come within its purview. The report power is, however, limited to corporations. In addition to its report power, the FTC has subpoena power whereby it can issue civil investigative demands (CID's)—a form of a subpoena—to require oral testimony of witnesses, written responses to questions, and/or the production of documents.

The FTC thus has very broad investigatory powers. The powers embodied in its CID authority permit it to issue formal subpoenas against third parties as well as anyone who is the target of an investigation. The subpoena may be issued as long as the information sought is relevant to the scope and purpose of the investigation being conducted by the FTC. FTC subpoena power includes natural persons as well as corporations.

If you should receive an FTC subpoena, you would naturally have any of the constitutional rights that you would have on the receipt of any other subpoena. The most likely right you might exercise is that concerning self-incrimination. It is available only to individuals, and not to corporations.

Other rights that might be asserted are the attorney-client privilege and the attorney work product privilege if the documents or information sought fell within those privileges. Those matters would need to be discussed with your attorney, and your accepting his handling of the situation would be extremely advisable and practically mandatory.

### Sources of information to initiate an investigation

The sources from which the Bureau of Competition receives information related to possible antitrust violations are similar to those used by the Antitrust Division. Through its various offices, the Bureau may receive complaints from customers, competitors, suppliers, and consumers regarding possible anti-trust violations. It may also receive information from other federal or state agencies, including a state antitrust enforcement section. It may initiate investigations based upon its own observations or experience or upon in-house economic studies. The studies may be prompted by earlier complaints or observations.

The Bureau of Economics may assist in reviewing conduct in certain industries or involving certain products. It may prepare economic studies, compile data and surveys, and analyze the data to determine whether economic theory indicates further inquiry.

As mentioned in the section on the Antitrust Division, you may have occasion to contact the FTC regarding a possible violation that you have observed or that you feel is damaging your company competitively.

### Informal investigations

The FTC, through one of its regional offices or through the Washington office, may on an informal basis by letter or personal contact inquire about certain conduct or ask for certain documents. You are not required to talk with FTC representatives or turn over any documents. However, it would be wise to consult with your attorney immediately. You might wish to cooperate rather than force the FTC to decide on whether to issue a subpoena for the same information.

It may be possible to prevent any further contact by convincing the Bureau of Competition, through interviews and documents, that your company is not engaged in any anticompetitive conduct that might be under investigation. The Bureau may not be investigating your company; it may only be seeking information related to one of your suppliers, competitors, or customers.

That is one obvious question that you would like answered before you provide any information to the FTC. Usually, the FTC will advise you upon contact what, generally, it is reviewing. The comments may be very general, but they will give you some guidance. However, even if the Commission represents that it is not presently investigating your company and you should voluntarily or in response to a subpoena turn over to it any documents or other information that is evidence of anticompetitive activity, then it could use that information against you.

Once you become aware of an investigation, it is extremely important that you be cautious about what records are destroyed. Although, arguably, you may continue your normal record destruction policy if no formal subpoena or request for information or report has been issued against you or your company, it is wiser to halt the normal destruction of any documents related to the area or products covered by the investigation. If a CID or request for information or report has been issued and/or you are aware of an investigation and destroy pertinent documents, you may be held in contempt of court or charged with obstruction of justice and be subject to certain fines and penalties.

When you provide documents or information, you must provide all the documents and information sought. In other words, you should not provide half-truths, give misleading statements, lie or falsify, alter, destroy, withhold, or in any other way fail to produce all of the documents within your custody and control and called for by the request or CID. To do so would subject you to possible fines and imprisonment.

See Informal Investigations under the discussion of the Antitrust Division earlier in this chapter for other pertinent comments.

## Civil antitrust investigation; use of civil investigative demands

The FTC, through its Bureau of Competition, can issue civil investigative demands to get information related to an investigation. CID's have the same force and effect as subpoenas. They can be issued to obtain information by oral testimony and/or document production from natural persons, corporations, partnerships, or any other entity. They can seek information from third parties (customers, suppliers, competitors) as well as targeted companies; the authority is very broad. The CID powers of the Antitrust Division and the FTC are very similar. See Civil Antitrust Investigation; Use of Civil Investigative Demands under the discussion of the Antitrust Division earlier in this chapter for other pertinent comments.

## Resolution of litigation

If a complaint has been filed against your company by the Federal Trade Commission, you have two choices: to attempt to work out a settlement (a consent order) or to litigate. If you attempt to settle, the FTC will generally require some form of consent order. Under the order your company will not admit any antitrust violation, but it will agree not to engage in certain conduct in the future (irrespective of whether the conduct occurred in the past) or to enter into certain types of agreements such as acquisitions. It may also agree to some form of restructuring, as of a distribution system, or whatever will, in the eyes of the FTC, correct the alleged violation or at least lessen its impact in the future.

You have no right to enter into a consent order, and any agreement on the consent order will be the result of negotiating a resolution of the litigation. Once a consent order is signed, it must be published in the *Federal Register* along with the reasons for accepting the consent order rather than further litigation. The FTC or the court must review and determine the order's adequacy. If the order satisfies the review, it will be approved and entered.

If you litigate, the first level is a hearing before an administrative law judge who listens to evidence from all parties and ultimately makes a ruling, including findings of fact and of law. The ruling can be appealed to the FTC itself, which reviews the administrative law judge's opinion and recommended order. The Commission can make its own findings of fact and law. The final order of the Commission can then be appealed to the U.S. Circuit Court of Appeals.

The usual although not exclusive remedy for the FTC is a cease and desist order requiring the defendant not to engage in the type of conduct in question. The order can be issued against individuals, such as officers and employees of a corporation, as well as the corporation itself for violating the antitrust laws.

The cease and desist order, in addition to enjoining activity similar to that coming within the allegations of the complaint, may also provide for restructuring of the corporation, divestiture of certain assets of the corporation, compulsory licensing of patents or trademarks, requirements to furnish technical information to others, and prohibition against future acquisitions within a particular line of business or industry. Violations of a final cease and desist order are punishable through civil contempt proceedings in the U.S. District Court. A penalty of $10,000 per violation is possible, and each day is considered a separate violation.

#### Other regulatory authority and procedures

*Trade Regulation Rules.*[5] The FTC can issue a trade regulation rule applicable to a particular industry, product, or type of conduct. Geographically, the rule can apply nationally or be more limited in scope. Its purpose generally is to prevent or correct conduct that is anticompetitive or harmful to unwary consumers and is believed to be occurring in a particular industry or to involve a particular product. A trade regulation rule is generally considered to have the force and effect of law, and any violation of a rule is considered similar to an antitrust violation. Enforcement proceedings are held by the Commission, and a $10,000 per day fine is possible.

To promulgate a trade regulation rule, the FTC must follow certain procedures. It must permit everyone interested in the proposed rule to comment and supply information. It must publish notice of the proposed rule in the Federal Register unless everyone subject to it is personally notified. In its discretion, it may hold oral hearings. Sometimes the hearings are held in various parts of the country with an administrative law judge or member of the Commission staff hearing the testimony. Interested persons may appear and testify in support of or in opposition to the proposed rule or offer an amendment to it.

The Commission is required to consider all relevant facts and law and any relevant matter presented by interested persons. It will make its decision based on facts derived from studies, reports, investigations, hearings, and any other proceeding. Any result is to be published in the *Federal Register.* The rule generally becomes effective 30 days after its publication.

A person can petition the Commission to issue, amend, or appeal a rule. The Commission is then required to consider the proposal and determine whether there is sufficient reason to initiate the rule-making procedure set forth above.

*Advisory Opinions.*[6] A business can seek an advisory opinion from the FTC on the legality of certain conduct that it is considering. The opinion does not have the force of law, and it does not bind the FTC, which can revoke or modify it upon notice to the applicant. The FTC will not give an advisory opinion on a hypothetical question if similar conduct is presently under investigation by the FTC or if it is or has been the subject of a current proceeding involving the FTC or another governmental agency or if it requires extensive investigation, testing, or inquiry to make a determination.

Trade and professional associations often make use of

advisory opinions of the FTC and business review letters of the Antitrust Division. That is especially true in areas of proposed exchange of information among members, surveys to be conducted among members, proposed membership restrictions, and any other prospective activity that might spark an enforcement agency's interest. It's often better to know now than later. Individual businesses also seek advisory opinions, again to clarify potential antitrust concerns.

As is true of most business decisions, the decision to seek an FTC advisory opinion has both advantages and disadvantages. The primary advantage is that you will have the FTC's position on certain proposed conduct that may have been unclear to you. The primary disadvantage is that the FTC will become aware of the proposed conduct and may give an adverse opinion. You would then need to decide whether to proceed anyway. The advisory opinion is just that—an opinion of the FTC. Any final resolution of the legality of the proposed conduct would be through the administrative and judicial processes.

The request for an advisory opinion must be specific and must contain detailed information. The FTC may request additional information, may conduct its own investigation of the facts, and/or may have conferences with the applicant and its attorney regarding the information submitted or requested by the FTC staff.

The FTC, naturally, may take a long period of time to reply. Therefore, if you plan to seek an advisory opinion, it is preferable that you submit the request well in advance of the anticipated beginning of the conduct in question. It is also important to be aware that the FTC generally will make public the request, its opinion, and all information provided to it except for trade secrets or customers' names and certain other commercial and financial information. Therefore, if you have information that falls within those categories and submit it to the FTC, you should request prior to submission that it be kept confidential.

*Industry Guidelines.*[7] An industry guideline is promulgated by the FTC for a particular industry or conduct within an industry. It does not have the effect of law; primarily, it gives the Commission's position on the competitive aspects of certain activities within the industry. Thus it is generally considered to have less legal weight than a trade regulation rule. The FTC may conduct investigations, studies, or hearings to determine whether to issue an industry guideline. It may initiate the review of a proposed industry guideline either on its own or pursuant to a petition from an interested person or group.

The issuance of an industry guideline can be helpful to a particular industry in that it puts the industry on notice that the FTC has taken a position pertaining to certain conduct within that industry. That, however, is a double-edged sword. The identification of the conduct can also provide for increased litigation in the area covered by the guideline if a company's conduct varies from that set forth in the guideline. At the least, the result can be closer surveillance of the industry. Since the industry guideline does not have the effect of law and, in effect, is merely the opinion of the FTC as to what would be deemed anticompetitive conduct, any suit filed by private parties alleging similar conduct as being anticompetitive and in violation of the antitrust laws or a suit filed by the FTC itself would still have to be litigated in order to be resolved.

### Authority to petition for cancellation of a trademark[8]

The FTC has authority to petition the Commissioner of Patents for the cancellation of a trademark under certain conditions. Various FTC representatives have stated that the FTC plans to use its authority to seek such cancellation more often in the future. If the FTC continues its policy of seeking new and "more effective" remedies, it may indeed do so. Some of the conditions for cancellation that may be pertinent to anticompetitive conduct are:

1. If the registered mark becomes the common descriptive name of an article or substance.
2. If the mark has been abandoned.
3. If the mark was fraudulently obtained.

4. If a registrant permits use of the certification mark for purposes other than to certify.
5. If the registrant refuses to certify goods or services of any person who maintains the standards or conditions which the mark certifies.

The FTC may initiate proceedings before the Commissioner of Patents, or an individual may petition the FTC to do so. If the FTC determines that there may be justification, it will initiate the proceedings.

### How to register an antitrust complaint with the FTC

You should contact the Bureau of Competition at either its Washington office or one of its regional offices (see Appendix B) if you have an antitrust complaint that you want to file with the FTC. It may be more helpful to pursue the complaint with the regional office. You can also file a complaint with the Bureau of Competition's Washington office at the same time or, if nothing is being done by the regional office, then sometime later. (See How to Complain to the Antitrust Division under the discussion of the Antitrust Division for other pertinent comments.)

### Private right of action under the FTC Act

The FTC Act gives enforcement responsibility and authority only to the Commission; it does not provide for any private right of action for an alleged violation of the Act. In other words, if particular conduct is considered to have violated the Act and caused damage to a particular person, that person has no cause of action, that is, no right to file suit and claim damages. As a practical matter, however, much of the conduct covered by the FTC Act is also covered under other federal antitrust laws that do provide the damaged individual with a cause of action.

### State and local antitrust enforcement activities

Most states have antitrust statutes and are becoming more active in enforcing them. Some states have given their attorneys general precomplaint investigative authority. The authority varies in extent from state to state, but it is generally similar in form to the civil investigative demand (CID) authority given to the Antitrust Division and the FTC. In addition, many of the states have criminal penalties for violation of their antitrust laws and provide for grand jury investigations.

It would be very unwise to shrug off the state antitrust laws or to feel your company is too small or too large to be involved or concerned. Without question, more and more states are becoming more and more active. Sometimes the Antitrust Division or FTC will turn a possible violation over to a state if it pertains primarily to that state and/or deals with firms located in the state.

The increased interest and activity in state antitrust enforcement is reflected in Congress, which in 1977 provided funding to the states of up to $10 million per year for 3 years strictly for antitrust enforcement. Congress has also required the Attorney General, through the Antitrust Division, to notify a state attorney general of an action under the antitrust laws that he has reason to believe would be cause for action by the state also. To the extent permitted by law and if requested by the state attorney general, the Antitrust Division must turn over any investigative files or other materials which are or may be relevant or material to the actual or potential federal antitrust cause of action if that will assist the state attorney general in evaluating the bringing of federal antitrust action.

Many state attorneys general have set up antitrust sections and staffs to concentrate on state antitrust matters. What conduct violates a state antitrust statute varies, but any activity that would violate the federal antitrust laws most likely would violate a state antitrust statute also. In addition, since no interstate commerce requirement must be met under the state statute, an activity that is purely intrastate in nature could be violative of the state antitrust laws. The damage provisions of a state statute can vary from single to treble damages, and most state statutes provide for private damage recovery. Some statutes also provide for local enforcement, which increases the number of agencies with antitrust enforcement authority.

Generally, the staff of a state antitrust section uncovers

possible violations in the same manner as the Antitrust Division and the FTC. In addition, it often works closely with the federal enforcement agencies. For example, several states, along with the Antitrust Division's regional offices, are experimenting with a hot-line telephone system with which the public can call in any complaints of anticompetitive conduct. Some of the antitrust sections have economists on their staffs or use consultants to assist them.

The staff of the antitrust section varies with budget, commitment, and the length of time the section has been in existence. The role of a state antitrust section is primarily twofold: to enforce the state antitrust laws and to recover damages suffered by the state, or its citizens as purchasers, as the result of alleged violations of the federal antitrust laws.

If representatives of a state attorney general's office contact you, consult your attorney before you talk with them, provide them with any information, or turn any documents over to them. He can best advise you of the attorney general's authority and your rights and help you determine the extent of your voluntary cooperation with the enforcement agency. A review of the comments under the discussion of the Antitrust Division can be helpful; it is appropriate to dealings with a state or local antitrust enforcement agency also.

### REFERENCES

1.  26 Federal Register 3555 (Apr. 24, 1961), Executive Order 10936.
2.  18 U.S.C. sec. 1001.
3.  15 U.S.C. secs. 1311–1314.
4.  CCH Tr. Reg. Reports, No. 354, p. 2 (October 10, 1978).
5.  16 CFR secs. 1.7–1.20.
6.  16 CFR sec. 1.1 et. seq.
7.  16 CFR secs. 1.5, 1.6.
8.  15 U.S.C. secs. 1051–1127 (the Lanham Act).

# 12

# Exemptions
# to the antitrust laws

There are certain limited exemptions to the federal antitrust laws. Some of them cover particular industries, and others cover particular conduct. Some are statutory, and some are derived from case law interpretation. All exemptions are generally narrowly construed by the courts and held to their specific areas. The apparent trend in case interpretation is to continue the narrow interpretation. This chapter gives you a brief summary of each exemption area.

## Regulated industries

Several industries are regulated by federal agencies: for example, securities and commodities, common carriers, communications, banking, airline (although it is being deregulated), and natural gas. Several other industries are regulated under state laws; they are discussed later in this chapter under State Action and State Regulation.

In most situations it would be fair to assume that conduct regulated by a federal agency is exempt from antitrust coverage. However, it is also fair to say that a regulated industry is exempt from antitrust coverage only to the extent that the industry is regulated. In other words, if the conduct in question is not one that would come within the scope of regulation, it is likely that a court would find it to be subject to antitrust scrutiny.[1]

Each regulated industry and each regulatory statute must be individually scrutinized whenever a question arises. Generally, the courts will look at the extent of the regulation, the role of the regulatory agency, the conduct in question and whether it explicitly or only implicitly falls within statutory coverage, and whether the federal agency should first review the conduct in question to see if it falls within the agency's jurisdiction and is permitted under its regulations. (The latter is often referred to as the question of primary jurisdiction.)

Although much conduct may obviously be covered by regulation by a federal agency, other conduct may only implicitly be covered. Even if a particular rule has been implemented by a federal agency, it is not necessarily consistent with the regulatory statute. This area, like many other areas of the antitrust laws, is complex. It is advisable to consult your attorney whenever you have any antitrust concern over certain company conduct even though your company is in a regulated industry.

Likewise, any deregulation of a particular industry would have to be reviewed to determine the extent of deregulation, over what time period, and for what conduct. Only in that way can you attempt to determine the extent of coverage of the antitrust laws. Review and analysis are especially important if your company is in an industry that was formerly regulated and is now becoming deregulated. Certain conduct that was previously permissible under a regulation umbrella may, upon deregulation, become a violation of the antitrust laws. An example is joint use of rating bureaus to determine fees.

### Agricultural cooperatives

Agricultural cooperatives are exempt from antitrust scrutiny by two federal statutes.[2] Basically, the statutes authorize persons engaged in agricultural production to act together in associations to collectively process, handle, and market products of persons so engaged.

An interpretation has been that an agricultural co-op can not join with an outside party to restrain trade through price fixing, limiting production, or any other such conduct.[3] In addition, the statute provides that the Secretary of Agriculture may order a cooperative to stop if it is found to be monopolizing or restraining trade "to such an extent that the price of any agricultural product is unduly enhanced."[4]

Questions that need to be answered in particular fact situations are whether the conduct in question is within the processing, handling, and marketing of agricultural products and whether the parties claiming the exemption are within the definition of a "person" engaged in production of agricultural products. In order for the cooperative to qualify for the exemption, all members must qualify as "farmers, ranchmen, dairymen, nut or fruit growers."[5]

If you have any questions as a member of an agricultural cooperative or as a customer, contact your attorney.

### Labor

Organized labor is exempted from antitrust coverage by several federal statutes,[6] but there are certain limitations. One is that the union can not join with an employer to restrain trade outside the scope of the union's normal activities. For example, an agreement between the union and an employer to restrict competition from others with the employer's product was found illegal as a violation of the federal antitrust laws. The union had obtained agreements from electrical contractors to use only equipment manufactured by companies having labor contracts with the union. The court held that the union lost its exemption when it entered into such agreements.[7]

Likewise, small businesses can not join or form a union in the hope of bargaining better as a group on the sale of their products. The U.S. Supreme Court has said that the labor exemption does not apply to disputes upon which the employer-employee relationship has no bearing.[8]

### Insurance

The "business of insurance" is exempt from antitrust coverage to the extent regulated by state law and to the extent the conduct is not a boycott or act of coercion or intimidation. (Such

conduct does not come within the exemption, and so it is subject to the Sherman Act.)[9]

Litigation has revolved around the definition of
"business of insurance" and whether particular conduct is a
boycott or act of coercion or intimidation. Naturally, each fact
situation is different. See Boycott of Competitors—Concerted
Refusals to Buy or Sell, Chapter 4, for a general overview of
boycotts.

### State action and state regulation

State action regulating the economic activity of an industry is
generally exempt from coverage of the federal antitrust laws,
and conduct of a company in complying with the state regulatory laws will generally be exempt from antitrust scrutiny. The
exemption is often referred to as the *Parker v. Brown*[10] doctrine. In recent cases the U.S. Supreme Court has so narrowed
the doctrine that it now requires a court to look at the extent of
state involvement in the regulatory process, the extent of the
state interest in the particular regulating process being reviewed, and whether there is a conflict with the federal antitrust policies. If there is a conflict, the court will need to balance the competing interests and determine which should
prevail.

For example, an electric utility company that provided
light bulbs to its residential customers without additional
charge was held not to be exempt from antitrust review of the
program even though the state's public utility commission had
to approve a program discontinuance.[11] There the involvement
of the private utility in determining the light bulb program was
dominant as compared with the state's regulatory requirements
on free light bulbs.

The point is that even though there may be a state statute
or a state agency's regulation that covers your activity, all conduct of your company will *not* automatically be exempted from
antitrust scrutiny. If the conduct in question is not part of the
state's regulatory policy, is approved only by an official
(without statutory authority), is broader than the authorizing
statute, or is really individual action camouflaged as state ac-

tion, it may be deemed a violation of the antitrust laws if, but for the supposed state regulation, it would be violative of the antitrust laws.

In addition, any activity entered into by a state or local government entity that would be considered of a proprietary or commercial venture rather than a government venture will not confer any exemption on the agreement or conduct involved. For example, the operation of an electric utility system by a local government agency would fall within coverage of the federal antitrust laws and anticompetitive conduct would be reviewed under the antitrust laws.[12]

### Petitioning the government (Noerr-Pennington Doctrine)

Joint effort to influence public officials or to lobby for particular legislation, even if directed against one's competition, is not within the Sherman Act. The U.S. Supreme Court was concerned that such activity might violate the first amendment to the U.S. Constitution, which permits petitioning the government. This is often referred to as the "Noerr-Pennington Doctrine."[13] Use of the administrative and judicial processes also is exempt, and that applies to both federal and state processes.

All of the above activity is exempt only as long as it is not a sham. That is, if the claim of petitioning the government or use of the administrative or judicial processes is really just an attempt to cover efforts to abuse the process (especially the administrative and judicial processes through filing of false or spurious claims) in order to accomplish an anticompetitive goal, it will be struck down. For example, abuse of the appeal process to keep a competitor tied up in hearings and filing new claims with the accompanying drain of resources and stamina may not come within the Noerr-Pennington Doctrine.

The extent to which the sham exception will apply is yet unclear. However, the more closely your conduct fits within the mold of petitioning your government through the legislative or executive branches, or proper exercise of your rights in using the administrative and judicial processes, the more likely the sham exception will not apply.

## REFERENCES

1. See, for example, *Silver v. New York Stock Exchange,* 373 U.S. 341(1963).
2. 15 U.S.C. sec. 17(1973) (sec. 6 of Clayton Act); 7 U.S.C. sec. 291(1964) (Copper-Volstead Act).
3. *Maryland & Va. Milk Producers Assn. v. United States,* 362 U.S. 458(1960).
4. 7 U.S.C. sec. 292(1973).
5. *National Broiler Marketing Assn. v. United States,* 436 U.S. 816(1978).
6. 15 U.S.C. sec. 17(1973) (sec. 6 of Clayton Act); 29 U.S.C. sec. 52(1973) (sec. 20 of Clayton Act); 29 U.S.C. sec. 101, 104, 105(1973) (Norris-LaGuardia Act).
7. *Allen Bradely Co. v. Local 3, IBEW,* 325 U.S. 797(1949).
8. *Columbia River Parkers Assn. v. Hentory,* 315 U.S. 143(1942).
9. 15 U.S.C. secs. 1101-15(1970). This is known as the McCarran-Ferguson Act.
10. 317 U.S. 341(1943).
11. *Cantor v. Detroit Edison Company,* 428 U.S. 579(1976).
12. *City of Lafayette v. Louisiana Power & Light Co.,* 435 U.S. 389(1978).
13. *Eastern Railroad President's Conference v. Noerr Motor Freight, Inc.,* 365 U.S. 127(1961); *United Mine Workers v. Pennington,* 381 U.S. 657(1965).

# 13

# Private antitrust actions

Throughout this book references have been made to the right of a private party to bring an antitrust suit in the event of injury by an antitrust violation. In this chapter several terms and concepts that are important to know and that relate primarily to private actions will be discussed. The rule of prima facie evidence is discussed in Chapter 3, and the discussion will not be repeated here. However, please review that discussion, because the rule of prima facie evidence can play a major role in private antitrust litigation.

Many questions are often raised when a party attempts to assert a private cause of action under the antitrust laws. Questions include whether the party has been "injured" as defined under the antitrust laws, whether the party can represent a "class" of similarly situated persons, the extent of joint and several liability of the defendants, and how many years back a plaintiff can go to collect damages.

## Joint and several liability

The courts have interpreted the federal antitrust laws as providing that a defendant is jointly and severally liable for damages suffered by any private party as a result of a violation of the federal antitrust laws by that defendant.[1] That is, if several defendants conspired and violated the antitrust laws and various plaintiffs suffered damages and can prove liability and recoverable damages, then each defendant is liable for all of the damages as trebled and each plaintiff can choose to collect its judgment from any one defendant or from some or all.

Of course, the plaintiff can collect only the total amount due it, but it can choose from whom to collect the trebled damages. Thus if a defendant goes bankrupt or is near insolvency, the other defendants are still liable to the plaintiff for the total amount of the trebled damages even if that one defendant can not contribute any share. Also, each defendant is liable for recoverable damages suffered by a plaintiff who dealt with only one of the other defendants, even though that plaintiff did not deal with the first defendant, as long as both defendants were involved in the conspiracy that caused the plaintiff the recoverable damages.

Assume, for example, that companies A, B, and C have engaged in a conspiracy to fix prices of product 100. The customers of each seller of product 100 were as follows:

> Company A has customers W and X
> Company B has customers W and Y
> Company C has customers W and Z

All four customers have suffered recoverable damages as a result of the price fixing of product 100 (that is, by buying product 100 at the fixed price) and have sued all three companies. Customer X has suffered $100,000 in damages. Any one of the three coconspirators A, B, and C is liable for the damage to X, even though only company A sold product 100 to X. Also, the liability is for treble damages, or $300,000.*

Likewise, customer W, which purchased product 100 from all three defendants, is entitled to attempt to collect its trebled damages from any one of the three defendants. If it has

---

*There is a conflict among the lower courts as to whether a plaintiff can seek damages for purchases made of the same product from non-coconspirator suppliers. The argument for such recovery is that the conspiracy caused all prices to rise above the competitive level. The U.S. Supreme Court has not yet resolved this conflict. See *Mid-West Paper Products Co. v. Continental Group, Inc., et al.,* 596 F. 2d 573 (3rd. Cir. 1979).

suffered $100,000 in damages, it can thus attempt to collect the trebled amount of $300,000 from one, two, or all three defendants.

Some courts have held that antitrust coconspirators do not have a right to collect a pro rata share of any judgment paid by a coconspirator from any other coconspirator. For example, if judgment is rendered for $1 million and trebled to $3 million and the plaintiffs attempt to collect the entire judgment from one defendant, that defendant does not have the right to receive a pro rata contribution from any of its coconspirators for a "share" of the judgment paid by it. However, certain other courts have held that there is a right of contribution among coconspirators, and thus the present status of right of contribution among coconspirators is uncertain.[2]

## Statute of limitations; stay; fraudulent concealment

The federal antitrust statutes provide that a person injured as a result of a violation of the antitrust laws can bring a private action to recover treble damages resulting from such conduct as long as the suit is filed within 4 years of the time the conduct occurred. If, for example, your company were a victim of price fixing and had last purchased the price-fixed product on June 29, 1980, it would have until June 28, 1984 to file suit to recover damages for that purchase. But, if your company did file on June 28, 1984, it would not be able to collect for damages prior to June 29, 1980, because the statute of limitations would have run out on all prior purchases unless it had been stayed in some manner or your company was successful in showing "fraudulent concealment" of the violation.

The statute of limitations is stayed, according to the federal statutes, during the period of any federal government enforcement action and one year after the termination of that action. That includes both criminal and civil enforcement cases. It does not include a government suit to collect damages allegedly suffered by the United States as a result of an antitrust violation. It does include suits by either the Federal Trade Commission or the Antitrust Division of the Department of Justice, and it also includes the typical injunctive relief suits filed by the Antitrust Division as companion cases to the criminal suits. Therefore, a delay in resolving a government enforcement suit extends the right of private parties to bring suit against the defendant. That is a factor to consider in attempting to resolve an enforcement action.

If the alleged violation was concealed from, or was unable to be ascertained by, the plaintiffs (called fraudulent concealment), then the statute of limitations on the damages claimed does not begin to run until the violation was, or should have been, known to the plaintiffs. For example, if a price fix on the sale of widgets has been in existence from 1960 to the present and the government today brings a criminal indictment against various of the widget vendors, the plaintiff's rights under the antitrust laws are not limited to damages within the past 4 years but can go back to damages suffered since 1960. A proviso is that the plaintiff must show it had neither knowledge nor any reasonable way of acquiring knowledge of the price fix until the announcement of the government's suit.

If your company is a defendant, then it may have plaintiffs alleging that the conduct was fraudulently concealed and that they can therefore seek damages stemming from activity which occurred more than 4 years before the date of the filing of the suit. An allegation of fraudulent concealment is more applicable in the case of a conspiracy such as price fixing, which would have been concealed, than, for example, in the challenge of a franchise agreement more than 4 years old. The challenged provisions of the franchise agreement would have been known to the parties for longer than 4 years.

### Class actions; notices of participation

When a private cause of action is filed, the plaintiff may attempt to represent all the other persons, including business entities, that are similarly situated and that could have suffered damages similarly to the plaintiff as a result of the alleged anticompetitive conduct. This *class,* if certified to exist as one by the court, is entitled to have its damages included in and is entitled to a share of any favorable judgment or settlement.

Also, the class is bound by any adverse ruling or findings including a judgment in favor of the defendants.

If, for example, a plaintiff sues for damages from an alleged price fix of hobnobs, it may ask to represent a class of all purchasers of hobnobs who might have been damaged. If the class is certified by the court to be represented by the plaintiff, then the court will require notice to those who, by definition, might fall within the class. The notice will generally advise each recipient about the suit and the certified class, and the recipient can "opt out" of (withdraw from) the class if it wishes by written notice to the court within a specified period of time. If, however, the recipient does not opt out, it will be bound by whatever the end result of the litigation may be. Thereafter, the recipient cannot bring its own suit on the same allegations against any of the defendants.

The names of the recipients are generally obtained from the defendants' customer lists or some other appropriate source. The U.S. Supreme Court has ruled that the plaintiff representative must bear the costs, at least initially, of the accumulation of the names and the sending out of the notices.[3]

If a settlement between a class and any defendant is proposed, the court will review the proposal. It will consider any facts and arguments presented at that time to determine preliminarily the adequacy of the settlement from the viewpoint of the class. If preliminary approval is given or a judgment is awarded in favor of the plaintiff and the class, another notice will be sent asking for purchase information to determine the allocation (after deduction of expenses and attorneys' fees) of the net proceeds of the settlement or judgment.

In the event of a settlement, the notice will also generally advise of a hearing date, on which any class member can argue against or in favor of the adequacy and fairness of the settlement. All settlements, expenses, and attorneys' fees must ultimately be approved by the court, which has a duty to protect the interest of the class. Any judgment in favor of defendants or plaintiffs and the class or any settlement ultimately approved by the court will be the sole determinant of what a class member can receive. The net proceeds after attorneys' fees, experts' fees, and miscellaneous expenses are distributed on some formula basis to the various class members.

Therefore, if you receive a notice of a class action suit, whether it be an antitrust action or any type of suit, you should read it carefully to determine the allegations of the suit and the date by which you must decide whether to opt out or remain in the class. You may wish to remain in the class and be represented either by the attorneys representing the class or by your own attorney, and generally the notice will discuss how to proceed.

You may wish to opt out for any number of reasons. Perhaps your company will file its own suit with the expectation of receiving a more satisfactory settlement for its alleged damages, or perhaps it just does not want to be a part of that particular litigation for business or other reasons. Typically, however, you must take an affirmative step to remove yourself from the class.

If you remain in a class and a settlement or favorable judgment is obtained, your company will again receive a notice. Again it will need to take affirmative steps, this time to provide purchase data to substantiate any claim it might make against the net proceeds. The notice should spell that out. Again, watch the timing deadlines.

### Parens patriae suits by states

State attorneys general have the right, under a federal antitrust statute, to sue for treble the damages suffered by natural persons residing in their states as the result of alleged violations of the Sherman Act.[4] The statute provides that an attorney general can sue on behalf of a natural person residing in a state but excludes business entities.

Generally then, the representation will primarily be of consumers within a state. If the state attorney general brings an action, he can do so on behalf of the state itself in an attempt to collect damages suffered by the state as a purchaser and also on behalf of the natural persons within the state. The statute does not create any new substantive antitrust rights, but it does authorize the state attorney general to represent the natural persons within the state without having to meet certain procedural requirements of a class action.

In a *parens patriae* suit, notice of the suit must be given to each person for whom the suit is filed. Unless the court orders otherwise, the notice may be by publication. Persons are then given an opportunity to opt out just as under a class action suit. Any settlement must be approved by the court, and the court must approve the method of allocating and distributing the funds among the potential recipients. If there are no claimants, the damages may be deemed a civil penalty and deposited in the state's general revenue fund.

### Recoverable injury

Section 4 of the Clayton Act provides that "any person who shall be injured in his business or property by reason of anything forbidden in the antitrust laws may sue" for treble damages. Thus a private plaintiff in a treble damage action must show that (1) the defendant(s) violated the antitrust laws (liability), (2) the illegal conduct involved caused the plaintiff damage to its business or property (fact of damage), and (3) the amount of the damage.

The courts have generally concluded that not all damages traceable to an antitrust violation are necessarily recoverable. The fact of damage (sometimes called "impact" of damage) must meet certain tests, such as a showing that the damages resulted "directly" from the antitrust violation or that the plaintiff was within the "target area" of the violation.

It is important to understand that, irrespective of what test is applied in a particular antitrust case, one of the three requirements to be met by a private plaintiff is fact of injury. Until then, no award of damages can be made by the court to the plaintiff.

Section 16 of the Clayton Act provides that "any person . . . shall be entitled to sue . . . against threatened loss or damage by a violation of the antitrust laws" and can sue for injunctive relief. Thus a plaintiff in an injunction suit need show, not actual damage, but only "threatened loss or damage."

## REFERENCES

1. See, for example, *Chattanooga Foundry & Pipeworks v. City of Atlanta*, 203 U.S. 390(1906); *Solomon v. Houston Corrugated Box*, 526 F. 2d 389, 392 n. 4(5th Cir. 1976).
2. See *Professional Beauty Supply, Inc. v. National Beauty Supply, Inc., et. al.*, 594 F. 2d 1179 (8th Cir. 1979).
3. *Eisen v. Carlisle & Jacquelin*, 417 U.S. 156(1974).
4. 15 U.S.C. sec. 15(c).

# 14

# Implementation of an antitrust compliance program

Is some form of an antitrust compliance program necessary?
Yes. What if your company is a small company? The program
is still a financial necessity. In fact, the overall financial risk is
greater if your company is small and does not have some form
of antitrust compliance program. The reason is that a government antitrust investigation and/or litigation or a private treble
damage suit could create financial ruin for a small company.
The cost of the investigation and/or litigation in lost employee
time, expenses, and attorneys' fees and any ultimate judgment
could become so great that a small company either cannot
afford to resist the investigation and/or litigation or may liter-
ally be forced into financial disaster because of it.

Naturally, the larger your company the more likely it is
to need a formalized and structured compliance program. A
small company may find a less structured and more informal
compliance program adequate. As long as the program is accomplishing its purpose—to keep the company from violating
the antitrust laws—then it is a good program whether it is
formal or informal.

No matter the size of the company, it is important that
top management actively endorse compliance with the antitrust laws. It certainly does no good to lecture on antitrust

compliance and then end the presentation with a wink. Likewise, it is the actions of top management rather than company policy statements that are more often followed by employees. Therefore, top management must implement the antitrust compliance policy of the company through its own actions and demands upon the other employees.

By review of the following discussion of a sample antitrust compliance program, you can determine the extent to which your company can implement its own program. No matter what the program, it is important to have an antitrust attorney assist management in setting it up. The attorney should be in a position to identify substantive areas that are most likely to involve your company and suggest methods of reviewing the areas of possible concern.

### Management endorsement

Any antitrust compliance program needs top management endorsement. Therefore, one of the first steps is issuance of written policy affirming the company's position to comply fully with the antitrust laws. The document might also include a statement to the effect that any employee found participating in an antitrust violation may be subject to dismissal, that each supervisor is responsible for his or her employees, and that all costs and expenses attributable to any antitrust litigation shall be allocated to the profit center involved.

The policy statement should be made available to and its receipt should be acknowledged by employees at all levels of the company organization who might be in a position to create antitrust concern for the company. Included should be all corporate management executives; top management of each division, operating center, profit group, or department; plant managers; sales, purchasing, and credit personnel; marketing personnel; employees with pricing authority; and employees who negotiate licenses, franchises, joint ventures, acquisitions, or dispositions.

In addition to the policy statement itself, the company should furnish some form of written source material to the various management personnel and others as a ready reference. Although in theory it would be most beneficial to have the employee contact the attorney on every antitrust concern, in practice that will not happen. Therefore, it is important that the employees have written material to give them a basic understanding of the antitrust areas and to answer some of the day-to-day questions. It might be a summary of the antitrust laws prepared by the company's attorney or a more extensive source such as this book. Whatever it is, it is a necessary part of an effective program. The company also needs to set up a way to provide each new affected employee with the company's policy statement and the antitrust source material.

## Company audit

There should be an antitrust audit of the various divisions, operating centers, departments, and/or profit groups to determine whether there is an indication of antitrust problems. The audit should be conducted by an attorney or by management in conjunction with an attorney, either an in-house or outside attorney. The attorney is in a better position to recognize possible antitrust problems from a legal standpoint.

The audit should be conducted in two phases: an initial review and a subsequent follow-up review. The initial review should cover documents, transactional information, and business conduct. The follow-up review should cover areas that raised an antitrust question during the initial review.

The initial review should include a review of documents such as license agreements, distributor agreements, and exclusive purchase or sales contracts. It should also cover sales policies, resale price policies, market strategies, research and development projects, price increases, and documentation on meeting competitors' prices.

The transactional information and business conduct to be initially reviewed should include the use of patents, purchases made from the company's customers, methods used to determine prices, and methods used for submission of bids, as well as decisions to discontinue a product line and to enter or leave a particular market. It should also include areas such as who has pricing authority, who has purchasing authority, and trade association involvement.

The follow-up review should cover areas that raised an

antitrust concern such as evidence of price exchange with competitors (for example, competitor price sheets in files), reasons for geographic differences in prices, reasons for sudden increases or decreases in prices, new or unusual market strategies, new or unusual sales policies, and sudden changes in any of the general terms of sale offered by the company for a particular product or group of products. It should also cover review of areas such as evidence of a tying arrangement; any sudden changes in the industry as a whole; reasons for termination of a particular dealer or supplier; any complaints from customers, suppliers, distributors, competitors, or franchisees; and any internal documents referring to "dominating the market," "killing our competition," "driving the competitors out of this area," or "teaching them a lesson for lowering prices" (or "for coming into our territory").

### Company seminars

There should be an annual antitrust seminar within the company or within each division, operating center, or profit group. It should be presented by an attorney with visible endorsement by top management, and it should be attended by any and all personnel who are in a position to place the company in antitrust problems.

It may be necessary to have different seminars at different times for different groups of employees. It is usually more convenient and practical to tie the antitrust seminar in with other meetings or gatherings of a group such as the sales personnel of a particular division or all the managers. That often has the added advantage of emphasizing the importance of antitrust compliance, since it ties in with other areas of emphasis and concern by the company. It might be impractical to have annual seminars for all personnel covered, and the company will have to determine, with assistance from counsel, the practical number and frequency of and attendance at seminars.

The seminar presentation can be made with the use of any lecture aids available, such as slides, charts, diagrams, summaries, handouts, and videotape. It should apply the coverage of the antitrust laws to activities of the company or the particular division, operating group, profit center, or department. It should not be a mere presentation of general antitrust theories with an underlying admonition to "always do the right thing." It must be real to have any impact upon the audience, whose members must be able to apply it to their daily work schedule.

The seminar most likely should be begun by pointing out all of the possible adverse consequences to both the employee and the company of a violation of the antitrust laws. Next to be pointed out are the purposes of the antitrust laws, that there are federal and state antitrust laws, and that the prohibitions are directed at anticompetitive conduct.

The substantive areas to be covered depend, to some extent, upon the length of time available and the nature of the business involved. Generally, however, the areas to cover include the per se violations of price fixing and allocation of markets, territories, or customers and the vertical concerns involving distributor or franchise relationships, tie-in of two products, and refusals to deal. There may also be areas of particular application to the company.

Next, a discussion of internal memoranda, documentation of certain activities, and contact with competitors would be appropriate. A discussion on internal memoranda might emphasize the danger of using loose language in internal memos, such as "we'll drive company X out of business," "we'll retain our dominant position in the market at any cost," or "we'll teach that [new entrant] a lesson." The discussion should cover the need for documenting price changes to meet a competitor's price to a customer, sudden changes in prices or in any other term of sale, changes in competitive position in the market, and any decisions on entering or not entering a new geographic, customer, or product market. A discussion on competitor contacts should emphasize no exchange of price lists or other competitive information and the need for caution in attending trade association meetings at which competitors are in attendance.

The seminar should wind up by emphasizing that anyone who has any question about antitrust impact should call the attorney. Open communication with the attorney is very healthy and should be emphasized. Most likely it is not practical to have each and every employee call with each question, but some system for accomplishing the communication should be set up and be called to the attention of the audience.

The seminar can end with a question-and-answer period. Typically that can become very time-consuming, and sufficient time for it should be allotted. It gives the attorney and management a first opportunity to hear what antitrust questions the audience has and how well the presentation has sunk in, and it emphasizes the much needed communication between attorney and employee.

The seminar program should be an ongoing program and be presented annually, if practical.

### Program individuality

The above program is merely a sample, and it has many variations. The size of a company, its product and people, and the ingenuity of the attorney and top management will dictate the variations appropriate for your company. A small company most likely could not afford such an extensive program; a very large company might find it extremely difficult to conduct effective annual audits. Emphatically, though, each company must keep management and other employees continuously aware of potential antitrust dangers. The program for doing so depends upon you and your company.

# Appendix

# A

# Pertinent parts of federal statutes

## SHERMAN ACT[1]

1. Every contract, combination in the form of trust or otherwise, or conspiracy, in restraint of trade or commerce among the several States, or with foreign nations, is declared to be illegal. Every person who shall make any contract or engage in any combination or conspiracy hereby declared to be illegal shall be deemed guilty of a felony, and, on conviction thereof, shall be punished by fine not exceeding one million dollars if a corporation, or, if any other person, one hundred thousand dollars or by imprisonment not exceeding three years, or by both said punishments, in the discretion of the court.

2. Every person who shall monopolize, or attempt to monopolize, or combine or conspire with any other person or persons to monopolize any part of the trade or commerce among the several States, or with foreign nations, shall be deemed guilty of a felony, and, on conviction thereof, shall be punished by fine not exceeding one million dollars if a corporation, or, if any other person, one hundred thousand dollars or by imprisonment not exceeding three years, or by both said punishments, in the discretion of the court.

[Remainder of Act has been omitted]

## CLAYTON ACT[2]

### [Section 1 has been omitted. Section 2 is under Robinson-Patman Act]

**3.** That it shall be unlawful for any person engaged in commerce, in the course of such commerce, to lease or make a sale or contract for sale of goods, wares, merchandise, machinery, supplies or other commodities, whether patented or unpatented, for use, consumption or resale within the United States . . . , or fix a price charged therefor, or discount from or rebate upon, such price, on the condition, agreement or understanding that the lessee or purchaser thereof shall not use or deal in the goods, wares, merchandise, machinery, supplies, or other commodities of a competitor or competitors of the lessor or seller, where the effect of such lease, sale, or contract for sale or such condition, agreement or understanding may be to substantially lessen competition or tend to create a monopoly in any line of commerce.

**7.** That no corporation engaged in commerce shall acquire, directly or indirectly, the whole or any part of the stock or other share capital and no corporation subject to the jurisdiction of the Federal Trade Commission shall acquire the whole or any part of the assets of another corporation engaged also in commerce, where in any line of commerce in any section of the country, the effect of such acquisition may be substantially to lessen competition, or to tend to create a monopoly.

No corporation shall acquire, directly or indirectly, the whole or any part of the stock or other share capital and no corporation subject to the jurisdiction of the Federal Trade Commission shall acquire the whole or any part of the assets of one or more corporations engaged in commerce, where in any line of commerce in any section of the country, the effect of such acquisition, of such stocks or assets, or of the use of such stock by the voting or granting of proxies or otherwise, may be substantially to lessen competition, or to tend to create a monopoly . . . [Remainder of Act omitted].

## ROBINSON-PATMAN ACT[3]

**2.**(a)  It shall be unlawful for any person engaged in commerce, in the course of such commerce, either directly or indirectly, to discriminate in price between different purchasers of commodities of like grade and quality, where either or any of the purchases involved in such discrimination are in commerce, where such commodities are sold for use, consumption, or resale within the United States or any Territory thereof or the District of Columbia or any insular possession or other place under the jurisdiction of the United States, and where the effect of such discrimination may be substantially to lessen competition or tend to create a monopoly in any line of commerce, or to injure, destroy, or prevent competition with any person who either grants or knowingly receives the benefit of such discrimination, or with customers of either of them: Provided, That nothing herein contained shall prevent differentials which make only due allowance for differences in the cost of manufacture, sale, or delivery resulting from the differing methods or quantities in which such commodities are to such purchasers sold or delivered: Provided, however, That the Federal Trade Commission may, after due investigation and hearing to all interested parties, fix and establish quantity limits, and revise the same as it finds necessary, as to particular commodities or classes of commodities, where it finds that available purchasers in greater quantities are so few as to render differentials on account thereof unjustly discriminatory or promotive of monopoly in any line of commerce; and the foregoing shall then not be construed to permit differentials based on differences in quantities greater than those so fixed and established: And provided further, That nothing herein contained shall prevent persons engaged in selling goods, wares, or merchandise in commerce from selecting their own customers in bona fide transactions and not in restraint of trade: And provided further, That nothing herein contained shall prevent price changes from time to time where in response to changing conditions affecting the market for or the marketability of the goods concerned, such as but not limited to actual or imminent deterioration of perishable goods, obsolescence of seasonal goods, distress sales under court process, or sales in good faith in discontinuance of business in the goods concerned.

(b) Upon proof being made, at any hearing on a complaint under this section, that there has been discrimination in price of services or facilities furnished, the burden of rebutting the prima facie case thus made by showing justification shall be upon the person charged with a violation of this section, and unless justification shall be affirmatively shown, the Commission is authorized to issue an order terminating the discrimination: Provided, however; That nothing herein contained shall prevent a seller rebutting the prima facie case thus made by showing that his lower price or the furnishing of services or facilities to any purchaser or purchasers was made in good faith to meet an equally low price of a competitor, or the services or facilities furnished by a competitor.

(c)  It shall be unlawful for any person engaged in commerce, in the course of such commerce, to pay or grant, or to receive or accept, anything of value as a commission, brokerage, or other compensation, or any allowance or discount in lieu thereof, except for services rendered in connection with the sale or purchase of goods, wares, or merchandise, either to the other party to such transaction or to an agent, representative, or other intermediary therein where such intermediary is acting in fact for or in behalf, or is subject to the direct or indirect control, of any party to such transaction other than the person by whom such compensation is so granted or paid.

(d)  It shall be unlawful for any person engaged in commerce to pay or contract for the payment of anything of value to or for the benefit of a customer of such person in the course of such commerce as compensation or in consideration for any services or facilities furnished by or through such customer in connection with the processing, handling, sale, or offering for sale of any products or commodities manufactured, sold, or offered for sale by such person, unless such payment or consideration is available on proportionally equal terms to all other customers competing in the distribution of such products or commodities.

(e)  It shall be unlawful for any person to discriminate in favor of one purchaser against another purchaser or purchasers of a commodity bought for resale, with or without processing, by contracting to furnish or furnishing, or by contributing to the furnishing of, any services or facilities connected with the processing, handling, sale, or offering for sale of such commodity so purchased upon terms not accorded to all purchasers on proportionally equal terms.

(f)  It shall be unlawful for any person engaged in commerce, in the course of such commerce, knowingly to induce or receive a discrimination in price which is prohibited by this section.

3.  It shall be unlawful for any person engaged in commerce, in the course of such commerce, to be a party to, or assist in, any transaction of sale, or contract to sell, which discriminates to his knowledge against competitors of the purchaser, in that any discount, rebate, allowance, or advertising service charge is granted to the purchaser over and above any discount, rebate, allowance, or advertising service charge available at the time of such transaction to said competitors in respect of a sale of goods of like grade, quality, and quantity; to sell, or contract to sell, goods in any part of the United States at

prices lower than those exacted by said person elsewhere in the United States for the purpose of destroying competition, or eliminating a competitor in such part of the United States; or to sell, or contract to sell, goods at unreasonably low prices for the purpose of destroying competition or eliminating a competitor.

Any person violating any of the provisions of this section shall, upon conviction thereof, be fined not more than $5,000 or imprisoned not more than one year, both.

## FEDERAL TRADE COMMISSION ACT[4]

### [Sections 1-4 are omitted]

5(a)(1). Unfair methods of competition in or affecting commerce, and unfair or deceptive acts or practices in or affecting commerce, are hereby declared unlawful. [Remainder of Act omitted]

## REFERENCES

1. 15 U.S.C. secs. 1–11.
2. 15 U.S.C. secs. 12–27.
3. 15 U.S.C. sec. 13.
4. 15 U.S.C. sec. 41 et. seq.

# Appendix
# B

# Field offices of the antitrust division and the FTC

## ANTITRUST DIVISION

New York (New York City): Connecticut, Maine, Massachusetts, New Hampshire, northern New Jersey, New York, Rhode Island, and Vermont.

Middle Atlantic (Philadelphia): Delaware, Maryland, southern New Jersey, Pennsylvania, and Virginia.

Great Lakes (Cleveland): Kentucky, eastern district of Michigan, Ohio, and West Virginia.

Midwest (Chicago): Denver, Colorado metropolitan area, Illinois, Indiana, Iowa, Kansas, western district of Michigan, Minnesota, Missouri, Nebraska, North Dakota, South Dakota, and Wisconsin.

San Francisco (San Francisco): Alaska, northern and eastern districts of California, Colorado (except Denver metropolitan area), Hawaii, Idaho, Montana, Nevada (except Las Vegas area), Oregon, Utah, Washington, and Wyoming.

Los Angeles (Los Angeles): southern and central districts of California, Arizona, New Mexico, and Las Vegas (Nevada) metropolitan area.

Atlanta (Atlanta): Alabama, Florida, Georgia, Mississippi, North Carolina, South Carolina, and Tennessee.

Dallas (Dallas): Arkansas, Louisiana, Oklahoma, and Texas.

## FEDERAL TRADE COMMISSION

Atlanta: North Carolina, South Carolina, Georgia, Florida, Alabama, Tennessee, Kentucky, Mississippi, and part of Virginia not covered by Washington, D.C. headquarters.

Boston: Maine, Vermont, New Hampshire, Massachusetts, Connecticut, and Rhode Island.

Chicago: Indiana, Illinois, Wisconsin, Minnesota, Iowa, and Missouri.

Cleveland: Ohio, Michigan, West Virginia, western New York, western Pennsylvania, and part of Maryland not covered by Washington, D.C. headquarters.

Dallas: Louisiana, Arkansas, Oklahoma, Texas, and New Mexico.

Denver: Colorado, Utah, Wyoming, Montana, North Dakota, South Dakota, Nebraska, and Kansas.

Los Angeles: Southern California and Arizona.

New York: New York (excluding the area west of Rochester) and New Jersey.

San Francisco: Northern California, Nevada, and Hawaii, with a branch office in Honolulu.

Seattle: Washington, Oregon, Idaho, and Alaska.

Washington, D.C. headquarters*: Washington, D.C., the Virginia cities of Alexandria, Falls Church, Fairfax, and Manassas; the Virginia counties of Arlington, Fairfax, Prince William, and Loudoun; the Maryland counties of Montgomery, Prince Georges, Howard, and Anne Arundel; and the counties in the Eastern Shore and southern section of Maryland.

*The Washington, D.C. office is the general headquarters of the FTC, but it also has responsibility for a geographic portion of the country.

# Index